# Life Skills Literacy

# Things to Know About Spending and Saving Money

by Richard S. Kimball
illustrated by Cecile Bayon

J. WESTON
**WALCH**
PUBLISHER
Portland, Maine

# User's Guide
## to
## *Walch Reproducible Books*

As part of our general effort to provide educational materials that are as practical and economical as possible, we have designated this publication a "reproducible book." The designation means that the purchase of the book includes purchase of the right to limited reproduction of all pages on which this symbol appears:

Here is the basic Walch policy: We grant to individual purchasers of this book the right to make sufficient copies of reproducible pages for use by all students of a single teacher. This permission is limited to a single teacher and does not apply to entire schools or school systems, so institutions purchasing the book should pass the permission on to a single teacher. Copying of the book or its parts for resale is prohibited.

Any questions regarding this policy or request to purchase further reproduction rights should be addressed to:

Permissions Editor
J. Weston Walch, Publisher
321 Valley Street • P.O. Box 658
Portland, Maine 04104-0658

1   2   3   4   5   6   7   8   9   10
ISBN 0-8251-3830-2

Copyright © 1998
J. Weston Walch, Publisher
P. O. Box 658 • Portland, Maine 04104-0658

Printed in the United States of America

# Contents

$$\$\$\$\$\$\$\$\$\$\$\$\$\$\$\$\$\$\$\$\$\$\$\$\$\$\$\$\$\$\$\$\$\$\$\$\$\$\$\$\$\$\$\$\$\$\$\$\$\$\$\$$$

# To the Teacher

$$\$\,\$\,\$\,\$\,\$\,\$\,\$\,\$\,\$\,\$\,\$\,\$\,\$\,\$\,\$\,\$\,\$\,\$\,\$\,\$\,\$\,\$\,\$\,\$\,\$\,\$\,\$\,\$\,\$\,\$\,\$\,\$\,\$\,\$\,\$\,\$\,\$\,\$\,\$\,\$\,\$\,\$\,\$\,\$\,\$\,\$\,\$\,\$$

*Things to Know About Spending and Saving Money* is another title in the growing *Life Skills Literacy* series from J. Weston Walch, Publisher. *Things to Know* books are reproducible and thematic compilations of information aimed at youth and adult English language learners, including ESL students new to American or Canadian culture. *Things to Know* books are intended to help build vocabulary, expand culturally-based knowledge, and develop real-life and survival skills. *Things to Know* books include interactive, authentic, cooperative, and idiomatic materials and activities. *Things to Know* books lead to success in the language and success in the classroom, the family, and the community.

The *Life Skills Literacy* series is appropriate for ESL learners at intermediate levels and for native learners reading at the fourth grade level and higher. Its vocabulary lists include more than 330 words and phrases, most of them specifically related to personal and consumer money matters like earning, spending, and saving. Illustrative and contextual clues offer assistance with lexical development. Verb forms are generally simple, and the use of passive voice is limited.

The pages of *Things to Know About Spending and Saving Money* and its companion books can help individual students build reading and writing proficiencies. They can help full classes and small groups of students develop speaking and listening competencies as well. They can help all learners understand personal money matters, and explore related subjects like taxes and banking.

Their brevity and focus make *Things to Know* titles excellent resources for tutors working with individual students, whether the books are also used in the classroom or not. Their basic level makes *Things to Know* suitable to a wide range of circumstances and student abilities. Their controlled language and high interest topics gives *Things to Know* appeal for students as well as teachers.

Like other *Things to Know* books, this one devotes three pages to each of 24 lessons. The first of the three is for teachers. It provides information and suggestions ranging from general concept considerations to specific Internet sites you and your students might visit. The second and third pages are reproducible, for student use. The second presents topic information and a dialogue, story, or student challenge relating to it. The third includes a word list plus writing and discussion activities for individual, small group, and full class use.

This book cannot cover all money-related vocabulary or all consumer topics of possible concern to students. Nor can it be designed to be exactly at the level of each and every student. But it can be and is very flexible, covering the basics at a consistently low reading level and then offering numerous ideas for moving beyond and providing extension activities to meet a wide range of classroom and personal needs. General ideas for materials use and adaptation appear on the following page of Teaching Suggestions. More specific suggestions can be found on the teacher page provided with each lesson.

We believe you will find the Walch *Life Skills Literacy* series and its individual *Things to Know* titles useful with many different students in many different settings. We'll be pleased to hear how well it works for you, to know what other titles you think should be added to it, and—as always—to learn what more this company can do to serve you and your students.

— *J. Weston Walch, Publisher*

# Teaching Suggestions

$ $ $ $ $ $ $ $ $ $ $ $ $ $ $ $ $ $ $ $ $ $ $ $ $ $ $ $ $ $ $ $ $ $ $ $ $ $ $ $ $ $ $ $ $ $ $ $ $ $ $ $ $ $ $ $ $ $ $ $

You can use *Things to Know About Spending and Saving Money* basically as is, having learners work through the two reproducible pages of each topic in one or two class sessions. Or you can make *Things to Know* the core of a broader approach to consumer and spending issues by following the many suggestions in the topical Teacher Pages and expanding each lesson to cover several sessions.

The first step in deciding how to use these pages is, of course, assessing the needs, interests, and abilities of your learners. The second step is considering the characteristics of your own community. Wherever you teach, you'll find that your classes benefit most when knowledge of local business and consumer resources are added to the *Things to Know* mix.

The "Preparation Possibilities" of the Teacher Pages provide some ideas of what you might wish to do in advance to enrich your classes, particularly if you are presenting a lesson over several class sessions. But these pages are designed for immediate use, and you need not spend hours preparing for their presentation. If you think local information will be helpful to your groups, follow the suggestions of the teaching pages and assign students to do the research. They will become true learners and enjoy themselves as well when they discover the practical value of outside projects. Or invite outsiders to join the class and talk about such complex matters as insurance.

Some of the "Technology resources" suggested on the Teacher Pages assume an Internet connection and use of a search engine to look for information and suggested Web pages.

Each word list contains between 12 and 15 terms. Those about money avoid the highly technical and should interest all wage earners and consumers. The more general terms are all important to the passages in which they occur, and have been selected with reference to readability levels and vocabulary frequency-use studies. In some cases, you may want to adjust the lists to help meet the needs and interests of your own students. You can underline the words you wish to stress, tape over those you don't want, and add others you find useful. But be careful not to eliminate terms required for the fill-in sentences that follow.

The idioms and slang and the "fascinating facts" given in the teacher pages are presented as fun and informative extras for some classes. If you use the idioms and slang, consider asking students to try them in sentences and to share other terms they know. You can treat the word lists in the same way, if you like, asking students to build sentences around them and to supply related vocabulary that interests them.

All materials on the Activity Pages have been prepared with references to varied thinking skills, learning styles, and the several intelligences proposed by Howard Gardner and others. But no mix can be perfect for every class, and these also can and should be adjusted to meet the needs of your own groups. The role plays based on dialogues, stories, and challenges is a useful example. Some students with very limited language skills will benefit from working in pairs and reading dialogues aloud to each other. More advanced students will enjoy and benefit from more creative approaches in which they make up their own parts and decide what might happen next to the characters in the story.

# Lesson 1: Spending Limits

## Themes

- Controlling expenditures
- Getting financial advice

**Background notes:** Economists sometimes debate whether the huge consumer debts run up in some Western countries are benign or not. But few doubt the consequences of large debts for individuals and families. They are often devastating. So this *Things to Know* package opens with pages you can use to help learners consider why they should hold spending within the limits imposed by income, and how they should do it. As most of us know from personal experience, that task is not easy. It can be especially tough for young consumers living on their own and filling entry-level jobs. Most of us do somehow survive even the lean periods, and in the process develop strategies and skills that can also work for others. So be sure and allow time in your classroom discussions for students to share the ideas that work well for them.

## Preparation possibilities

- Think about: financial planning courses and other resources available in your area
- Bring to class: appropriate books and articles on basic personal finances

## Technology resources

- Search topic: *personal finance* (for commercial sites, college courses by Web, etc.)
- Web pages to try: Consumer Information Center

## Student pages

- Page 2 includes: an introduction to spending limits and a dialogue in which two friends discuss personal spending problems

- Page 3 includes: a word list you may adjust for your class and student activities

**Especially for ESL:** Students new to American and Canadian cultures may need help knowing how much personal information most westerners are comfortable sharing. Tell them: Many people are willing to talk in general terms but not to share personal financial information. Ask: Was the same thing true in your first countries? What kind of financial advice could you get in those countries?

## Extra idioms and slang to introduce

- *Rolling in money/dough/it*: wealthy
- *Tight*: stingy; unwilling to spend money

**Thoughts to share with learners:** Some people define *maturity* as "the ability to postpone pleasure." Other terms for *financial counselors* include *financial planners*, *financial advisors*, and *financial planning consultants*.

**Questions to ask learners:** Who in the class sometimes feels broke? Who has some ideas for saving money? What do you do when you really want something you can't afford? Do you find that if you wait a few days you won't want it as much? Has anybody taken a local personal finance course? Was it good?

**Projects to assign learners:** Find the names of local financial consultants. Try the yellow pages, and share what you find with the class. Find out about personal finance classes. Do local schools offer them?

**A fascinating fact to share:** In 1997, the average American household spent 92.5 percent of its income.

# Lesson 1: Spending Limits

Are you very rich? So rich you have trouble just counting your money? Then you don't need to worry much about spending **limits**. The rest of us do. We have limited **resources**. We need to limit what we spend to what we have. If we don't, we use **credit** and get **in debt**. Then we need more money, and we spend more in the long run. Good spending is limited spending. That might sound simple, but it's a hard lesson for a lot of us to learn.

$$$$$$$$$$$$$$$$$$$$$$$$$$$$$$$$$$$$$$$$$$$$$$$$$$$$$$$$$$$$$$$$$$$$$$$

## Dialogue: A second job

**First Friend:** You look happy this morning. What's up?

**Second Friend:** I made a decision last night. I decided to get a second job.

**FF:** That makes you happy? It makes me tired just to think about.

**SF:** I'm broke. I need more money.

**FF:** What for? You've got all the **essentials** now.

**SF:** I want more than essentials. I want nicer clothes and a faster car. I want to buy a house.

**FF:** Maybe you need to spend less, not get into **real estate**.

**SF:** You want me to be some sort of **miser**?

**FF:** Fat chance! I just don't think you should be a **spendthrift**.

**SF:** But I want more stuff. Maybe I can win the **lottery**.

**FF:** It might rain money tomorrow, too. I don't think you need more money. I think you need better money **management**.

**SF:** I manage my money okay. I get it and I spend it.

**FF:** Maybe you should take a course in **personal finance**.

**SF:** I won't have time if I get a second job.

**FF:** Maybe you won't need the job if you take the course.

**SF:** What about you? I suppose you have all the money you want.

**FF:** Don't I wish. I'm in debt up to my ears.

**SF:** Then how come you're handing out advice?

**FF:** It's from an **expert**. I'm seeing a financial **counselor**.

**SF:** So what have you learned?

**FF:** She says I need to give up my **charge cards** and **take charge** of my money instead.

**SF:** Are you doing it?

**FF:** I'm trying. But it's not so easy.

**SF:** Maybe you need another job.

**FF:** Not that. But I do need a cup of coffee. Join me?

**SF:** I can't. I'm broke.

**FF:** That's okay. I've still got one charge card.

*Life Skills Literacy:*
*Things to Know About Spending and Saving Money*

# Lesson 1: Spending Limits

**$ ACTIVITY PAGE**

## Word list

| limit(s) | in debt | miser | management | counselor |
|----------|---------|-------|------------|-----------|
| resource(s) | essential(s) | spendthrift | personal finance | charge card(s) |
| credit | real estate | lottery | expert | take charge |

## Increasing your understanding

1. Look at the word list. If you don't know a word, find out what it means. Try to figure it out from the way it is used on page 2. Or look it up in a dictionary.

2. Supply the missing words from the word list:

(a) Many of us have limited _____ so we can't buy too much.

(b) If we use too much credit, we get _____.

(c) The second friend in the story wants to win the _____ and get more money.

(d) The counselor says people should give up _____, and _____ of their money instead.

(e) The second friend doesn't think the first friend should be a miser or a _____.

---

## Questions to discuss

1. Does one friend in the story need more financial advice than the other? Give reasons for your answer.

2. What are the "essentials" that the first friend talks about? Brainstorm a list of things that most people need to have.

3. What can you do if you don't have enough money to pay your bills?

## Things to write about

1. What if you won the lottery? What would you do first? Write a paragraph giving your answer.

2. Is buying lottery tickets a good idea? Write a letter giving advice to a friend who spends $25 a week on tickets.

## Things to do

1. Act out the story on page 2 with a partner. Use your own words if you want. Decide what the friends might say when they go for coffee.

2. How can people cut their costs? Make a list of at least five ideas.

3. Who needs a financial counselor? Make an illustrated newspaper ad for a counselor named Rich Saver. It should tell people how they can know if they need help.

4. Do most people think they have enough money? Ask five or more people outside class. Share what you find with your classmates.

*Life Skills Literacy:*
*Things to Know About Spending and Saving Money*

# Lesson 2: Budget Basics

## Themes

- Balancing income and expenses
- Getting financial advice

**Background notes:** Lacking a plan, too many people spend until the last paycheck is gone, then struggle through to the next, hoping fervently that no forgotten bills will arrive in the interim. Help your students to see that a more reasonable course is to budget. That means putting their plans on paper, not simply holding them in their heads and then adapting to the most pressing need of the moment. If you are presenting these pages in a school offering a full program, ask other teachers if they have presented your learners any information on budgeting, and adjust your presentations accordingly.

## Preparation possibilities

- Think about: the apparent spending needs of your students
- Bring to class: inexpensive budgeting guides and aids

## Technology resources

- Search topic: *budget* (for government, business information), *financial planning*
- Web pages to try: *Amazon.com* (and similar bookstore pages for print resources)

## Student pages

- Page 5 includes: an introduction to budgeting and a story about a group of friends budgeting for a shared rental apartment
- Page 6 includes: a word list you may adjust for your class and student activities

**Especially for ESL:** People new to western cultures may welcome information and reminders about matters most natives take for granted — allowing for sales tax, for example, and remembering April 15 as a tax deadline in the United States. Ask: Did schools teach about budgets in your first country? In the story, Sun talks about "essentials." What are they? Are "essentials" the same for everybody?

## Extra idioms and slang to introduce

- *Fork out:* pay money for something
- *Blow your money:* spend your money unwisely

**Thoughts to share with learners:** Budgets work only if they are both written and read. You can buy inexpensive books on budgeting at most bookstores.

**Questions to ask learners:** Who in the class has a written budget? Does it help you? Who has worked on a budget for a business or another organization, like a club? Is that a difficult job? Is it useful? What sorts of things can people share to save money? (In the story on page 5, some friends share an apartment.)

**Projects to assign learners:** Visit a library and look for books about budgeting. Begin some work on your own budget. Decide how much money you took in and how much you spent last week. Discuss the process with the class (but don't think you need to share private information about your own finances). Is it easy to do? Can you remember everything you spent?

**A fascinating fact to share:** Researchers say that disagreements about money are a major cause of divorce.

# Lesson 2: Budget Basics

Some people don't like **budgets**. They think budgets keep you from spending money. But budgets don't do that. Budgets are spending plans. They tell you what you can spend. They also help you **balance income** and **expenses**. And they can keep you out of debt. People who make spending plans are usually glad. Complicated plans are hard to follow. So if you make a plan, keep it simple. Then you will probably use it.

$$\$\$\$\$\$\$\$\$\$\$\$\$\$\$\$\$\$\$\$\$\$\$\$\$\$\$\$\$\$\$\$\$\$\$\$\$\$\$\$\$\$\$\$\$\$\$\$\$\$\$\$\$\$\$\$\$$$

## Story: A balancing act

Sun and seven friends wanted to share their expenses. They rented an apartment together and called it a **cooperative**.

They also wanted to share the work in their **co-op**. Sun was studying **accounting** in school, so he agreed to handle finances.

Sun called a meeting about money. He talked about **assets** and **liabilities**. He talked about accounting **principles**. "Do you have any questions?" he asked.

"Yes," said Tom. "What are you talking about?"

Sun's other friends were confused, too. After the meeting Sun asked Mara what to do.

"Think about the **KISS** principle," she said.

"What does kissing have to do with this?" said Sun.

"Nothing. This is a different KISS. It usually means 'Keep It Simple, Stupid.' But you aren't stupid. So this time it means 'Keep It Simple, Sun.' And explain the words you use."

Sun called another meeting. "Let's talk about a budget," he said. "That's a spending plan."

On a large sheet of paper he wrote "Money In" and "Money Out."

"To run our house we need to spend money," he said. "That's money that goes out. We use it for our liabilities or **expenditures**. I mean 'expenses.' That's the simpler word. If we have money going out, we need money coming in. That's our income. And that's what I meant by 'assets.'"

"The money in needs to equal the money out," said Sun. "They need to balance. If we spend too much, we go broke. We have to have **discipline** and we can't spend too much. We should have a little extra in case of trouble. That's our **reserve**."

"That sounds simple enough," somebody said.

"Yes, it is," said Sun. "Just like a kiss."

"What?" said Tom.

"Mara can explain in a minute," said Sun. "But first let's talk about our expenses."

*Life Skills Literacy:*
*Things to Know About Spending and Saving Money*

Name_____ Date _____

# Lesson 2: Budget Basics

## Word list

| | | | | |
|---|---|---|---|---|
| budget(s) | expense(s) | accounting | principle(s) | discipline |
| balance | cooperative | asset(s) | KISS | reserve |
| income | co-op | liabilities | expenditure(s) | |

## Increasing your understanding

1. Look at the word list. If you don't know a word, find out what it means. Try to figure it out from the way it is used on page 5. Or look it up in a dictionary.

2. Supply the missing words from the word list:

   (a) In the story on page 5, Sun and his friends called their apartment a "cooperative," or _____.

   (b) "You should think about the _____ principle," Mara said.

   (c) The group needed to have _____ and not spend too much, according to Sun.

   (d) Sun talked about assets and _____ and accounting principles at the first meeting.

   (e) Budgets help _____ income and expenses, according to the paragraph at the top of page 5.

## Questions to discuss

1. Is Sun a good person to handle the money in the story on page 5? Why or why not? What are some of the jobs his friends might do?

2. What do you think about co-ops? Brainstorm the good and bad points of living in one.

3. How would a co-op's budget compare to one person's budget? To the budget for a small business?

## Things to write about

1. Why should people make budgets? Write a paragraph giving your reasons.

2. What could go wrong in a co-op? What might the budget reserve in the story be used for? Describe one possible problem.

## Things to do

1. Act out the story on page 5. Play the parts of Sun and Mara, but use your own names if you want. Decide what job the person taking Mara's part will do in the co-op.

2. Make a chart like the one Sun started in the story. List some of the items that might go under "Money In" and "Money Out."

3. What's another word like KISS? With two or three classmates, make up another budget saying. Use words with first letters that make another short word.

4. Do most people have written budgets? Ask at least four people outside the class. Share your findings in class.

6

*Life Skills Literacy:*
*Things to Know About Spending and Saving Money*

# Lesson 3: Budget Categories

## Themes

- Building budget plans
- Tracking where the money goes

**Background notes:** "Where has our money gone?" is an all too common question. Complete answers are all too uncommon. Many people have little idea where their money goes, according to financial planners. Finding out is a reasonable starting point in financial counseling sessions for clients at every economic level and of every educational background. These pages are designed to give your students a head start in the process while also considering the budget categories they could use.

## Preparation possibilities

- Think about: budgeting categories that might be appropriate for your learners
- Bring to class: appropriate books or other sources with full personal or organizational budgets

## Technology resources

- Search topic: *consumer spending statistics*
- Web pages to try: U. S. Commerce Department, Census Bureau; Statistics Canada
- Software to consider: *Money*, CD-ROM for managing personal finances, from Microsoft; *Quicken*, CD-ROM for managing personal finances, from Intuit

## Student pages

- Page 8 includes: an introduction to budget categories and line items, and a challenge story about keeping track of expenses
- Page 9 includes: a word list you may adjust for your class and student activities; for

Activity 2 under "Things to Do" you might have students share their budget outlines but not financial data

**Especially for ESL:** Ask: Did you have a budget in your own country? What categories did you need? Are they different than the ones you need now?

## Extra idioms and slang to introduce

- *private eye:* detective
- *bread:* money

**Thoughts to share with learners:** Budgeting information needs to be kept safe and organized. A disorganized system can mean a disorganized budget.

**Questions to ask learners:** What might be in a personal budget in addition to what is in the box on page 8? (For one thing, it would show both income and expenses. This list of spending categories is based on one compiled by the American Financial Services Association and included in the *Consumer Adviser* published by Reader's Digest: Housing, Food, Transportation, Clothing, Health Care, Personal Care, Recreation, Gifts and Contributions, Savings, Obligations, and Education.)

**Projects to assign learners:** Keep a notebook or a calendar with you for one week. Write down every cent you spend. Are you surprised by how much you spend?

**A fascinating fact to share:** Governments spend about one third of all the money spent in the United States. The federal government's budget for 1999 added up to about 1.7 trillion dollars.

# Lesson 3: Budget Categories

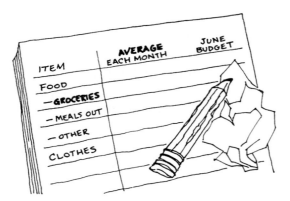

Here's how to make a monthly budget. First, decide what kinds of things you buy. Food and clothes are examples. Use these as **categories** in your budget. Under each category write the items you buy. You can call these **line items**. Next to each item, write the average amount you spend. That means the amount you usually spend in a month. Then write the amount you expect to spend this month. List all your items this way. Then add up what you plan to spend. Will you have enough money? If not, you need to make changes.

$ $ $ $ $ $ $ $ $ $ $ $ $ $ $ $ $ $ $ $ $ $ $ $ $ $ $ $ $ $ $ $ $ $ $ $ $ $ $ $ $ $ $ $ $ $ $ $ $ $ $ $

## Reader Challenge: A job for a detective

You are a private **detective**. You are sitting in your office one day when a man and woman visit. They want to hire you.

"Good," you say. "Because I can solve it." That's my **slogan**. 'I can solve it.' Now, what needs solving?"

"Our money is gone," they say.

"Who do you think took it?" you ask.

"Nobody," the husband says. "We spent it."

"Then you must know where it went."

"That's just the problem," the wife tells you. "We don't know where our money goes. So we can't make a budget. We can't build our **savings account**. We can't get ahead."

You know that a lot of people wonder where their money goes. Most don't hire detectives to find out. But you have your own bills to pay, and you want the job.

"What do you want me to do?" you ask.

Your **clients** want you to look at their bills, **receipts**, and **checkbooks** to see what they have spent in the past. They want you to follow them secretly to see what they spend in the future. They want you to help make a budget. And they want you to help them decide their **net worth**.

"I'm a detective, not an **accountant**," you say. "But net worth is easy. You just subtract what you owe from what you have. I can **analyze** your spending, all right. And I can make a budget without putting everything into the **miscellaneous** category. I'll take the case. I can solve it."

But when the couple leaves, you are nervous. You realize that you don't know where your own money goes. Maybe you should think about your own budget before you start somebody else's.

### Here's your challenge:
Think about your own expenses. List your own budget categories.

8

*Life Skills Literacy:*
*Things to Know About Spending and Saving Money*

# Lesson 3: Budget Categories

## Word list

| | | | | |
|---|---|---|---|---|
| average | line item(s) | savings account | checkbook(s) | analyze |
| groceries | detective | client(s) | net worth | miscellaneous |
| categories | slogan | receipt(s) | accountant | |

## Increasing your understanding

1. Look at the word list. If you don't know a word, find out what it means. Try to figure it out from the way it is used on page 8. Or look it up in a dictionary.

2. Supply the missing words from the word list:

   (a) The paragraph at the top of page 8 says food and clothes might be _____ in your budget.

   (b) You are a private _____ in the story on page 8.

   (c) You say you can make a budget without putting everything into the _____ category.

   (d) The couple can't make a budget or build their _____.

   (e) You are not an accountant, you say, but _____ is easy.

---

## Questions to discuss

1. How did you answer the challenge on page 8? What categories should your budget have?

2. What's the matter with *miscellaneous*? Why does the detective promise to make a budget without putting everything into the miscellaneous category?

3. Do you agree with the detective? Do you think a lot of people wonder where their money goes? Why?

## Things to write about

1. What would a detective find out about you? Imagine that a detective followed you yesterday. Write a report saying where the detective saw you spending money.

2. Imagine that you pay cash for oil to heat your house. Last year you paid a total of $480 for oil. That means you paid an average of $40 a month. Is that the amount you should budget for January? Write a paragraph saying why or why not.

## Things to do

1. Role-play the story on page 8 with another student. One of you can be the detective. The other can be a client. Decide if this is a good way to find out where your money goes.

2. What kind of spending plan will work for you? Make a one-month budget for yourself. Use the box on page 8 as a model. Put in as many categories and line items as you need. Be sure to include both income and expenses.

3. Why should you take a class in budgeting? Write a radio ad for a school that has a class in spending your money wisely. Tell people why they should join. Read your ad to the class the way you would read it on the radio.

4. Where do you keep your important financial papers? Do you have a safe, single place? If not, find one. Make a list of what should go in it. Share your ideas with the class.

*Life Skills Literacy:*
*Things to Know About Spending and Saving Money*

# Lesson 4: A Place to Live

## Themes

- Finding a good housing deal
- Types of housing

**Background notes:** The world of housing has a vocabulary of its own, a complicated one that bankers, lawyers, and real estate agents are paid well to understand. The rest of us may struggle with it whenever we make housing changes. But at least we can focus on the areas that interest us most. Apartment hunters don't need to think much about mortgages, and most home buyers don't have to worry much about landlord-tenant relationships. As you prepare for using these next two topics, consider how to narrow your presentation to the subjects that will most interest your own learners. That may differ greatly from one geographic area to another and from one class to another.

## Preparation possibilities

- Think about: the housing needs of your own students and the housing choices in your area
- Bring to class: sample housing ads, rental contracts, consumer guides on housing

## Technology resources

- Search topic: *tenant-landlord relations, housing, homelessness*
- Web pages to try: U. S. Department of Housing and Urban Development; consumer rights divisions or attorneys general of state, local, and provincial governments

## Student pages

- Page 11 includes: an introduction to searching for housing, and a dialogue between a home owner and prospective renter

- Page 12 includes: a word list you may adjust for your class and student activities

**Especially for ESL:** Members of ethnic minorities sometimes encounter discrimination in housing, and you might wish to use the dialogue on page 11 to discuss that subject. Ask: What should you do if you feel you are unfairly treated?

## Extra idioms and slang to introduce

- *A roof over your head:* a place to live
- *Rip-off:* fraud, bad deal

**Thoughts to share with learners:** One of the best ways to know if rental housing is good is to ask other people who live in it. If you need a lawyer, look for one you can afford. Some are reasonable, and will help people without a lot of money. Don't give up before you start.

**Questions to ask learners:** What are some of the things that can go wrong when you look for an apartment or a house? Does anybody know of good housing deals in this area? What is *subsidized housing* (housing that the government helps pay for)? Is it a good idea? Is there any in this area?

**Projects to assign learners:** Imagine that you are about to move. Use ads and friends to find out about good places. Call some to ask about rates. Discuss what you find with your classmates.

**A fascinating fact to share:** In 1990, the United States had 102 million housing units. About 1 million of them had incomplete plumbing, according to the census bureau.

# Lesson 4: A Place to Live

*(handwritten classified ad clipping)*
Call 102 W 211
**129. APARTMENTS & HOUSES TO SHARE**
GLENVIEW REALTY
**WANTED: M/F** to share 3 **BR** house. Completely furn. with **W/D**. I pay the **mortgage.** You pay **util.** **NS** only. Call 555-123-1234
131. ROOM
SUNNY
...responsible...

A good housing deal can improve your life, and that's worth working for. How can you use your housing money wisely? That's where the work comes in. Ads can be **misleading** unless you know the language of housing. If you don't know much about housing, **protect** yourself. Get a real estate agent to help find a good apartment or house. Don't sign papers you don't understand. Ask a lawyer to read them first. A lawyer might cost money. But a bad housing deal can cost a lot more.

$$$$$$$$$$$$$$$$$$$$$$$$$$$$$$$$$$$$$$$$$$$$$$$$$$$$

## Dialogue: Right on the water

**Home Hunter:** I'm calling about a place to live. My friend says you have one right on the water.

**Home Owner:** I sure do. But it's just a **seasonal**. Is a **short-term** rental okay?

**HH:** Sure. My friends and I are students. We just need it for the winter.

**HO:** That's good. I use it all the time in the warm weather.

**HH:** I'm out of town right now. Can you send me a description? And a copy of your **rental agreement**?

**HO:** Sure. But this place won't last long. Somebody's going to grab it fast. I'll need a **security deposit** soon if you want it.

**HH:** I understand. How many bedrooms does it have?

**HO:** Three. And they all look out on the water.

**HH:** That's just right. There will be me and two friends. And one of my friends has a daughter. They can share a room.

**HO:** How old is the daughter?

**HH:** She's three.

**HO:** Oh-oh. That's not so good. I can't rent to you after all.

**HH:** But you can't refuse us. You can't turn people down in this state because they have children. That's **discrimination**, and it's **illegal**.

**HO:** This isn't discrimination. This is common sense. My place is dangerous for little kids in high winds.

**HH:** Then it can't be much of a house.

**HO:** But it isn't a house. Just what did your friend tell you about it?

**HH:** He said it's a wonderful house built right on the water.

**HO:** I think you heard him wrong. This is a wonderful house *boat* right on the water. It's in the water, not near it. Still interested?

**HH:** A boat? I get seasick just thinking about boats. I've got to go. I'm sorry. Good-bye.

**HO:** Good-bye. And good luck!

*Life Skills Literacy:*
*Things to Know About Spending and Saving Money*

Name_____ Date _____

## Lesson 4: A Place to Live

### Word list

| | | | |
|---|---|---|---|
| M/F (male/female) | mortgage | protect | agreement |
| BR (bedroom) | util. (utilities) | seasonal | security deposit |
| furn. (furnished) | NS (nonsmoker) | short-term | discrimination |
| W/D (washer/dryer) | misleading | rental | illegal |

### Increasing your understanding

1. Look at the word list. If you don't know a word, find out what it means. Try to figure it out from the way it is used on page 11. Or look it up in a dictionary.

2. Supply the missing words from the word list:

   (a) The ad at the top of page 11 is for a three-bedroom house that's completely _____.

   (b) The ad says "_____" only. Don't answer it if you smoke.

   (c) If you don't know much about housing, _____ yourself, says the paragraph by the ad.

   (d) The home owner in the story needs a _____ soon if the caller wants to take the place.

   (e) Discrimination against people with children is _____, the caller says.

### Questions to discuss

1. Should the owner in the story rent to people with small children? Why or why not?

2. What do rental agreements say? How can you tell if one is fair? Brainstorm your answers.

3. Is it better for most people to rent a house or buy one? What about you?

### Things to write about

1. Would you like to live on a houseboat? Write a paragraph saying why or why not.

2. Can you get it fixed? Imagine that the washer in your apartment house doesn't work. Write a letter to the owner asking for repairs. The owner's name is Rita Renter.

### Things to do

1. Act out the story on page 11 with a partner. Decide what kind of house the caller should get.

2. How many kinds of housing are there? Apartments and houses are just two types. Make a list of at least five more.

3. What kind of house or apartment do you like? Draw a simple floor plan you could show a real estate agent.

4. Are the ads near you like the one on page 11? Look at some newspapers outside class. Make a list of some of the abbreviations in the ads. Then see if your classmates found anything different.

*Life Skills Literacy:*
*Things to Know About Spending and Saving Money*

# Lesson 5: Paying for Utilities

## Theme

- Controlling utilities costs

**Background notes:** Utility bills can come as unpleasant surprises, especially for people new to an area or living on their own for the first time. Even veteran apartment and home hunters sometimes forget to ask about utilities responsibilities and costs until after they have fallen in love with a promising new place. Some of your students may have learned these lessons the hard way and may be well-equipped to help others understand the information on these pages.

## Preparation possibilities

- Think about: utilities costs, practices and problems in your area
- Bring to class: sample utilities bills, pamphlets from local utilities

## Technology resources

- Search topic: *public utilities* (narrow by geographic area)
- Web pages to try: California's Public Utilities Commission (and similar sites in other areas)

## Student pages

- Page 14 includes: an introduction to utilities prices and a story about trying to cut electric bills
- Page 15 includes: a word list you may adjust for your class and student activities

**Especially for ESL:** People new to the United States and Canada may be unfamiliar with the concept of private payment for utilities. As the United States deregulates, ESL students may need extra help finding good deals and predicting the costs of utilities in rental units. Ask: How do utilities here compare to those in your first country?

## Extra idioms and slang to introduce

- *Chip in:* contribute money for something a group is buying
- *Pay through the nose:* pay too much

**Thoughts to share with learners:** In most states a Public Utilities Commission (PUC) or Public Service Commission (PSC) regulates utilities. These commissions decide what utilities can charge. And you can complain to them if you have a problem. A kilowatt-hour (KWH) is power equal to the work done by a thousand watts of electricity in one hour. Electric companies charge according to kilowatt-hours used. That's what the electric meters in buildings measure.

**Questions to ask learners:** When you rent an apartment, how can you tell how much utilities will cost? Who in the class works hard to save electricity, gas, and water? How do you do it? Why do Americans use so much of the world's energy (24 percent)? Will this ever change?

**Projects to assign learners:** Find out where your community's electricity and water come from. Are these sources close and cheap, or not? Find out the cost of residential electricity per KWH in your area. Use what you find in the math problem on page 15 (Activity 3 under "Things to Do.")

**A fascinating fact to share:** American consumers spend about 3.5 billion dollars every year to run electronic equipment like television sets. About 1 billion of that pays for power used by equipment that is turned off — like a VCR with a clock that keeps going.

# Lesson 5: Paying for Utilities

Natural gas. Water. Electricity. Phones. These are important utilities. They help us live the way we want. But they can cost a lot. The prices depend on where we live. Gas costs more in some places, less in others. The same is true for water and oil. But sometimes we pay more than we should. Companies can make mistakes. So we need to look at bills like this one very carefully. We shouldn't pay for more than we get.

## Story: Paying the bills

Raj and his friends had a party. They wanted to celebrate sharing an apartment for a whole year. But Colin was angry.

"Utilities!" he said. "Utilities are killing us!"

He picked up a paper from the table. "Look at this electric bill! It's even higher than last month's. I don't understand."

"I don't either," said Lenya. "How can the bill be high if it's always dark in here?"

"You're right," added Mara. "Tom keeps turning the lights off. Sometimes I can't even see to read."

"I'm just trying to save money," Tom told her. "Other people keep leaving the lights on. And paying these bills is driving me crazy!"

"Wait," said Raj. "Let's not be angry."

"I agree," Lenya told him. "This is really a good apartment. We like living together. We get along well with our **landlord**, and he likes us as **tenants**. That's good, because tenant-landlord **relations** are important."

She was right. The **lease** was reasonable, too. It cost much less than the **condo** the group

once thought about **subletting**. The apartment was great, except for the cost of utilities.

"The water bill is high, too," said Mara. "So is the phone bill, but it will go down when everybody pays for their own long distance calls."

"The next thing you know, Tom won't want us taking showers," Mara grumbled.

"Not true!" Tom said. "And this is a party. Let's have a good time! I even brought everyone presents."

He passed out packages to his six friends, and kept one for himself. Each contained the same thing — a **candle**.

"There!" said Tom. "Now we can have candlelight dinners every night. That will keep the electric bills down. It will even help heat the place so we won't need so much gas. Now let's light up our party!"

*Life Skills Literacy:*
*Things to Know About Spending and Saving Money*

## Lesson 5: Paying for Utilities

## Word list

| | | | |
|---|---|---|---|
| service center | KWH | landlord | sublet(ting) |
| account | (kilowatt-hours) | tenant | candle |
|  number | residential | relations | |
| previous | interest | lease | |
|  balance | delinquent | condo | |

## Increasing your understanding

1. Look at the word list. If you don't know a word, find out what it means. Try to figure it out from the way it is used on page 14. Or look it up in a dictionary.

2. Supply the missing words from the word list:

   (a) In the story on page 14, Lenya says that landlord-tenant _____ are important.

   (b) At the party, Tom gave a _____ to each of his friends.

   (c) The _____ was more reasonable than the one for the condo the group looked at.

   (d) The bill on page 14 says _____ is charged for _____ accounts.

   (e) According to the bill, the customer's _____ is 12345-54321.

## Questions to discuss

1. Do you think the friends in the story will stay in their apartment for another year? Give reasons for your answer.

2. Why are utilities costs so different? Why do people in some parts of the country pay less than others for utilities? Is this fair? Should the price be the same no matter where you live?

3. Should the price of heating oil go up? What would happen if it doubled? Would this be a good way to make people use less? Is that a good thing to do? Why?

## Things to write about

1. What if the lights go out? Write a paragraph saying how people should prepare for times when the electricity is off.

2. Imagine that you get a letter saying your electric account is delinquent. But you know you paid a month ago. Write a letter explaining this to Sparks Electric Company.

## Things to do

1. Role-play the parts of two friends from the story. Decide whether you think Tom's idea of using candles is a good one. Talk about some other ways to cut lighting costs.

2. What are some ways to cut electric costs in a shared apartment? List at least six ideas.

3. How much does it cost to dry clothes? Do this problem: Imagine that your dryer uses 5,000 watts of electricity. That means it uses five KWH if it's on for an hour. If electricity costs 13 cents a kilowatt-hour, how much does it cost to run the dryer for four hours? How much for a year if you use the dryer two hours a week?

4. Find some ways to save water in the place where you live. Try them, then share your ideas with your classmates.

*Life Skills Literacy:*
*Things to Know About Spending and Saving Money*

# Lesson 6: Shoppers' Choices

**Themes**
- Comparing retail grocery outlets
- Driving less to cut air pollution

**Background notes:** How many of us always use our food money wisely? Probably few of us have perfect records, because of the planning and organization required. But lots of us do fairly well, and helping students do the same is a reasonable goal. Discussions of grocery shopping can go in many directions, from health considerations to packaging. A useful starting point for many classrooms is local shopping options. These pages should help you and your learners begin thinking about such matters.

**Preparation possibilities**
- Think about: food shopping options and values in your area
- Bring to class: newspaper ads, information about food clubs and co-ops, other resources

**Technology resources**
- Search topic: *food* (for lots of resources, including electronic purchase possibilities)
- Web pages to try: U. S. Food and Drug Administration, Food Information Council Foundation

**Student pages**
- Page 17 includes: an introduction to the "Five W's for Shoppers," a challenge activity about the best place to buy groceries
- Page 18 includes: a word list you may adjust for your class and student activities

**Especially for ESL:** Students new to American and Canadian cultures may face the special challenge of finding foods familiar in their own countries. Ask: Do you miss some special foods from your native countries? Have you found good places to buy some of those items here?

**Extra idioms and slang to introduce**
- *Piece of change:* money
- *Mom-and-pop store:* business run by a couple or a family

**Thoughts to share with learners:** Huge food and other stores have made great changes for the United States, Canada, and other countries in recent years. Some people like the changes, but others do not. Time counts, too, when you decide what store to use. Sometimes you can save a lot by shopping close to home or by planning ahead when you go farther.

**Questions to ask learners:** Do you watch any television shows about people who live together and share jobs like shopping? How do they divide duties and settle arguments? Is buying in bulk a good idea? What can go wrong if you do that? Are the "Five W's" on page 17 a good idea? Can you think of another "W" to add? Another way to say the same ideas?

**Projects to assign learners:** Visit several stores to look at the price of rice. See how much you can save if you buy 10 pounds at a time instead of just one. (See also Activity 4 under "Things to Do" on page 18.)

**A fascinating fact to share:** According to *Consumer Reports* for May 1995, the average markup for supermarkets is 20 percent to 24 percent. The average markup in warehouse clubs is 10 percent.

# Lesson 6: Shoppers' Choices

FIVE **W**'s FOR SHOPPERS

**WHO**? Who wants it? Do they really need it?

**WHAT**? What is it? Will something cheaper do?

**WHERE**? Where are you going to get it?
—Is there a better, cheaper place?

**WHEN**? Is there a better time to buy it?

**WHY**? Why should you buy it? Can you borrow or rent or do without?

Do you always get the best buys? Most of us don't. We pay more than we need to. We buy at the wrong times. We get things we really don't need and won't use. One way to do better is to remember the Five W's for Shoppers. Another is to plan. This is important for food and other items. If you plan ahead you can **buy** food **in bulk**. You can make one big shopping trip instead of several short ones. Then you can drive to a large store where prices are low.

$$$$$$$$$$$$$$$$$$$$$$$$$$$$$$$$$$$$$$$$$$$$$$$$$$$$$$$$

## Reader Challenge: Where should you get it?

It's your turn to cook dinner. But you need to get a few things like milk, coffee, bread, salad **ingredients**, and meat. You tell your roommates that you are going out. You ask if they need anything.

Lennie wants rice for the next day's meal. Abbay says you need light **bulbs**.

That's good, you tell them. You can get everything at Chan's **Convenience** Store down the street. You won't have to drive anywhere.

"Oh, don't do that," says Lennie. "Go to the **supermarket**. Prices are cheaper there. You can get things in bulk and save us all some money."

"But if I go there I have to drive," you answer. "That's **inefficient**. It means paying for gas and adding to **pollution** and taking extra time."

"Forget about pollution," says Lennie. "Your little car doesn't do any harm next to all those truck and buses."

"But I should avoid gas **consumption** whenever I can. Besides, I want to support the Chan family," you say. "They offer a good **neighborhood** service. I want our money to go to them."

Then you ask Abbay what he thinks.

"I wouldn't go to either place," he tells you. "The **produce** at the supermarket stinks. You should see the **wilted** lettuce. And the meat isn't all that hot. I'd go to the **specialty** stores downtown. You know, the **butcher** for meat and the baker for bread. They aren't cheap, but you get your money's worth. Then stop by the farmer's market for **vegetables**."

You are afraid Lennie and Abbay will begin a long argument.

"Thanks for your advice," you say. "But I'm doing the shopping, so I guess I'll make the decision."

You head out the door. But you still don't know where you are going.

**Here's your challenge:** What's your choice? Where do you think you should shop?

*Life Skills Literacy:*
*Things to Know About Spending and Saving Money*

## Lesson 6: Shoppers' Choices

## Word list

| buy (something) in bulk | bulb(s) | inefficient | neighborhood | specialty |
|---|---|---|---|---|
| | convenience | pollution | produce | butcher |
| ingredient(s) | supermarket | consumption | wilt(ed) | vegetable(s) |

## Increasing your understanding

1. Look at the word list. If you don't know a word, find out what it means. Try to figure it out from the way it is used on page 17. Or look it up in a dictionary.

2. Supply the missing words from the word list:

   (a) The paragraph at the top of page 17 says you can _____ food _____ if you plan ahead.

   (b) In the story on page 17, Abbay says you should go to the _____ stores downtown.

   (c) You are worried about pollution. You want to avoid gas _____ whenever you can.

   (d) Lennie wants you to go to the _____ and save money.

   (e) When the story begins, you want to go to a _____ store down the street.

## Questions to discuss

1. How did you answer the challenge on page 17? Where would you shop? Is that the sort of place you usually go?

2. What would happen if everybody used neighborhood stores all the time? How would towns and cities change? Would there be less air pollution from cars?

3. Do big stores near you charge less than small stores for the same things? Why do you think there are differences?

## Things to write about

1. Do you like shopping for food? Write a paragraph saying what you like or don't like about it.

2. How can Chan's Convenience Store get more business? Write a slogan for the store. It should make more people want to shop there.

## Things to do

1. Role-play the story on page 17 with a partner. Take the parts of any two people in the story. Use your own names if you want. See if you can find a way to save money and gas.

2. What kind of places sell groceries? List at least eight. Include the ones on page 17 if you like.

3. Make a poster showing the five W's on page 17. Use your own words to explain the W's if you want. Illustrate the poster any way you like.

4. Where can you buy a pound of white rice for the best price? Look around in stores near you. Then share your findings with your classmates.

*Life Skills Literacy:*
*Things to Know About Spending and Saving Money*

# Lesson 7: In the Supermarket

## Themes

- Understanding supermarket sales approaches
- Good shopping practices

**Background notes:** The managers and marketers of supermarkets typically give more thought to buyer behavior than buyers do. Modern western stores may be loaded with values unknown in some parts of the world. But they are also loaded with messages and marketing tricks designed to separate shoppers from as much money as possible. These pages should help learners develop good shopping habits and find solid values in the supermarkets they visit.

## Preparation possibilities

- Think about: the supermarkets in your area
- Bring to class: newspaper ads, consumer guides to shopping (books like *The Consumer Bible: 1001 Ways to Shop Smart;* see also *Consumer Reports* articles on supermarkets, such as that in the issue of August 1997)

## Technology resources

- Search topic: *food cooperatives* (for alternate food sources)
- Web pages to try: Supermarket chains by name; The Center for Science in the Public Interest (information on nutrition)

## Student pages

- Page 20 includes: A drawing of a typical supermarket layout, an introduction to supermarket sales practices, and a dialogue about supermarket shopping

- Page 21 includes: A word list you may adjust for your class and student activities

**Especially for ESL:** Ask: How does food shopping in your new country compare to shopping in this one? Has confusion about English ever led to wrong and amusing selections?

## Extra idioms and slang to introduce

- *Come-on:* something designed to attract
- *The scoop:* information

**Thoughts to share with learners:** Jim is right (in the story on page 20). Supermarkets do make mistakes. So it's good to be sure the scanners at the checkout give the price you saw on the shelf. But it's a lot of work to keep track of all the prices, especially when you are buying many items.

**Questions to ask learners:** What's a house brand? (It has the store's name on it.) What's a name brand? (A famous, well-advertised brand) If the products are the same, which should you get? How can you tell if two products are the same? What time of day should you shop for food? (Not when you are hungry)

**Projects to assign learners:** As a class, choose an inexpensive item like pretzels. Do some comparison shopping to find the best prices. Then get a few bags and do a taste test. How do price and taste compare? Do an eye-level test of your supermarket. Look to see which products are at your own eye level. Which ones are on bottom shelves and hard to see? Which are at the right height for children to see?

**A fascinating fact to share:** In 1995, the average American household spent almost $4,300 a year on food.

# Lesson 7: In the Supermarket

Supermarkets can sell you lots of the things you need. Then they are great. But they also try to sell you lots of things you don't need. Then they aren't so great. How can you avoid **impulse buying**? One way is to understand how supermarkets work. Think about their design, for example. **Staples** like dairy products are at the back. People have to walk past lots of displays just to get a bottle of milk. Does your supermarket work like that?

$$$$$$$$$$$$$$$$$$$$$$$$$$$$$$$$$$$$$$$$$$$$$$$$$$$$$

## Dialogue: A long shopping trip

**First Friend:** It's late. Where were you?

**Second Friend:** At the supermarket with Jim.

**FF:** For three hours? But you had just a few things to get.

**SF:** Shopping isn't easy with Jim. I'll never go with him again.

**FF:** Why not? He's taken a **consumer education** course. He should be a great shopper.

**SF:** He's too good, believe me.

**FF:** What happened? Did you give into **temptation**? Did you do a lot of impulse buying?

**SF:** With Jim there? Are you kidding?

**FF:** Did Jim's **calculator** slow you down?

**SF:** It sure did. He checked the **unit prices** of everything. He checked 15 different cereals. He knows what they all cost **per ounce**.

**FF:** But there are signs for that.

**SF:** Jim didn't trust them. He said stores can make mistakes. So he checked every one. Then he compared all the **nutrition labels**. He knows how many **calories** every kind of jelly has.

**FF:** At least you learned about **comparison shopping**.

**SF:** I also learned about store layout from Jim. He kept talking about it. "Smell the fresh bread," he said. "That's near the entrance to build customers' **appetites**. And look at the milk. You need it every day. But it's at the back. You see every special display getting there."

**FF:** Did you get some good buys?

**SF:** I guess so. But we almost didn't get anything. Jim wanted to put it all back. When he added it up, he got a total of $336.23.

**FF:** For a dozen things?

**SF:** Yes. Jim made a mistake on his calculator. The total at the checkout was $27.39.

**FF:** I guess shopping is about more than dollars and cents. It's also about common sense.

**SF:** Yes. And common sense means not shopping with Jim again.

*Life Skills Literacy:*
*Things to Know About Spending and Saving Money*

# Lesson 7: In the Supermarket

## Word list

| | | | | |
|---|---|---|---|---|
| dairy | impulse buying | temptation | nutrition | comparison |
| product(s) | staple(s) | calculator | label(s) | shopping |
| display | consumer | unit price(s) | calories | appetite(s) |
| checkout(s) | education | per ounce | | |

## Increasing your understanding

1. Look at the word list. If you don't know a word, find out what it means. Try to figure it out from the way it is used on page 20. Or look it up in a dictionary.

2. Supply the missing words from the word list:
   (a) The drawing at the top of page 20 shows the _____ near the entrance of the supermarket.
   (b) The paragraph by the drawing talks about how to avoid _____.
   (c) "Did you give into _____?" asks the first friend.
   (d) Jim knows how many _____ every kind of jelly has.
   (e) He says the fresh bread near the entrance of the store will build customers' _____.

## Questions to discuss

1. Why does Jim think the store has fresh bread at the front? Do you think he's right?

2. Can calculators help you shop? How can you be sure you aren't making a mistake like Jim's? Brainstorm your answers.

3. Which sense is most important for stores? Taste? Smell? Hearing? Sight? Sound? Do supermarkets think of them all when they sell things? Give examples.

## Things to write about

1. Write a letter to Sarah's Supermarket. Ask to have the milk at the front where it is easy to get. Say how the change might help the store.

2. Should you always buy the product with the lowest unit price? Write a paragraph giving your answer and your reasons.

## Things to do

1. Role-play the story on page 20 with a partner. Decide how you can get Jim to speed up if you shop together again.

2. What if you build a supermarket? What questions should you ask? Make a list of at least five. Here's one you can use: How close are other supermarkets?

3. How can you sell a new cheese spread? Meet with three or four other students. Imagine that you all work for a supermarket. Decide what your store can do so customers will want the cheese spread. Then compare your ideas to what other student groups decide.

4. Do supermarkets near you look like the drawing on page 20? Look at two or three stores in your area. Then share what you find with your classmates.

*Life Skills Literacy:*
*Things to Know About Spending and Saving Money*

# Lesson 8: Saving on Clothes

## Themes

- Controlling clothing costs
- Buying used clothing

**Background notes:** Clothing offers an area of great potential savings to many consumers. Although it is possible to spend a fortune dressing oneself, it is also possible to dress inexpensively and well. These pages cover some of the approaches used to do this, like buying used clothing, shopping by the calendar, and using discount stores. You might wish to expand your presentation to cover others, such as making one's own garments and visiting manufacturers' outlets.

## Preparation possibilities

- Think about: inexpensive clothing outlets in your area and your own students' probable reactions to inexpensive clothing outlets
- Bring to class: information about good clothing sources in your area; consumer materials about clothing purchases

## Technology resources

- Search topic: *clothing* (also by garment type, manufacturer, or retailer)
- Web pages to try: The Apparel Strategist (industry information)

## Student pages

- Page 23 includes: An introduction to finding inexpensive clothes and a story about shopping in thrift stores
- Page 24 includes: A word list you may adjust for your class and student activities

**Especially for ESL:** People from other countries may need some assistance understanding clothing sizes in the United States and Canada. Some common resources contain conversion charts. For example, the book *Numbers*, written by Andrea Sutcliffe and published by Harper Perennial, gives United States, United Kingdom, and European equivalents. Ask: Does your native country have used clothing stores?

## Extra idioms and slang to introduce

- *Dressed to kill/to the teeth:* dressed very well
- *Lose your shirt:* Lose everything you have

**Thoughts to share with learners:** Pricing and advertising are closely related. "Designer clothes" are heavily advertised and very expensive. Consumers pay for ads, so if you want cheaper clothes, look for labels you don't see in ads. Some of these come from the same factories that make designer clothes.

**Questions to ask learners:** Who in the class has tried second-hand clothing stores? Have you found good ones? Where else can you get cheap clothes? (Discount houses, manufacturers' outlets, church rummage sales)

**Projects to assign learners:** Visit some used clothing stores in your areas. Share what you find with the class.

**A fascinating fact to share:** Women spend nearly twice as much as men on clothes ($607 a year compared with $345 in 1994, according to *Cut Your Spending in Half without Settling for Less,* by Rodale Press).

# Lesson 8: Saving on Clothes

Why pay full **retail** prices for clothes? You don't have to. You can find good used clothes at **thrift** stores and **consignment** shops. You can get new clothes by mail, or at **discount** stores. You can buy **irregulars**, **imperfects**, and **seconds**. These have minor problems. You probably won't even see them. You can save money at the mall, too. Go in January for winter clothes. Try in July for summer clothes. That's when stores are changing their **lines** for the next season.

$$$$$$$$$$$$$$$$$$$$$$$$$$$$$$$$$$$$$$$$$$$$$$$$$$$$$$$$$$$$

## Story: Dressing for success

Carla **convinced** Carlos to shop at the thrift store.

"You have to look nice for your **interview** on Monday," she told him.

"I'm embarrassed to shop at a thrift store," said Carlos. "All my friends get brand new clothes."

"I don't," said Carla. "Neither does my family. My mother once found $100 worth of clothes at a thrift shop for under $10. We don't buy expensive things just to **impress** our friends. That's called '**conspicuous** consumption.'"

Carla's family also shopped at consignment shops. "They make a **profit**," Carla explained. "So they're more expensive than the thrift stores. Those are usually run by **nonprofit organizations** like the **Salvation Army**. But the consignment shops are still cheap."

"Okay, okay," said Carlos. "I'll try it."

Carla went with Carlos on Saturday morning and pointed out a dressy blue shirt.

"It looks almost new," she said.

A heavy man standing near them smiled. "It is almost new," he said. "I brought it in last week because it doesn't fit me any more. I've gained some weight, so now I'm looking for larger sizes."

Carlos bought a belt, three pairs of pants, and two shirts.

"What do you think of thrift shops now?" Carla asked.

"They're great. As long as nobody I know sees me here."

Carlos looked sharp when he left for the interview Monday.

That afternoon, Carla saw him.

"I got it!" he said. "I got the job!"

"Great!"

"And guess why!"

"Why?"

"The man who hired me was the man we saw at the thrift shop Saturday. I was wearing his shirt. He was impressed that I shopped at a thrift shop. He said he wanted an employee who knows how to save money. And I'm it!"

"Thanks to the thrift shop," said Carla.

"Thanks to you," said Carlos. And he gave her a hug.

*Life Skills Literacy:*
*Things to Know About Spending and Saving Money*

## Lesson 8: Saving on Clothes

### Word list

| | | | |
|---|---|---|---|
| retail | irregular(s) | convince(d) | profit |
| thrift | imperfect(s) | interview | nonprofit |
| consignment | second(s) | impress | organization(s) |
| discount | line(s) | conspicuous | Salvation Army |

### Increasing your understanding

1. Look at the word list. If you don't know a word, find out what it means. Try to figure it out from the way it is used on page 23. Or look it up in a dictionary.

2. Supply the missing words from the word list:

    (a) The paragraph at the top of page 23 asks why people pay full _____ prices for clothes.

    (b) Three words used for clothes with minor problems are _____, _____, and _____.

    (c) In the story, Carla says that thrift stores are run by _____.

    (d) Carla's family doesn't buy expensive things just to _____ their friends.

    (e) Carlos wanted to look nice for his _____ on Monday.

---

### Questions to discuss

1. Is Carla right? Does she convince you that thrift stores and consignment shops are good places to get clothes?

2. Why do some people care so much about expensive sneakers and other clothes? Are such things important to you? Why or why not?

3. Do Carla's ideas about clothes work for other things? What else can you get that's imperfect? That's used? Brainstorm your answers.

### Things to write about

1. What should you look for in clothes? How can you tell good from bad? Write some advice that a friend could use.

2. Imagine that you buy some used pants. In the pocket is a brand new $100 bill. What will you do? Write a paragraph giving your answer.

### Things to do

1. Act out the story on page 23 with a partner. Use your own words if you want. Then role play the part of Carlos and his new boss. One of you interview the other. Then switch parts.

2. When are clothes important? You have to wear special clothes for some jobs. Write a list of five jobs like that, and tell what kind of clothes you need.

3. Can you get people to use your consignment shop? With three or four other students, make a TV ad for Connie's Consignment Shop. Then present the ad to your class. The ad should convince people that used clothes are good. All the members of your group should be in it.

4. Can you find used clothing stores in your area? Make a list of those you find outside of class, then share it with your class.

*Life Skills Literacy:*
*Things to Know About Spending and Saving Money*

# Lesson 9: Thoughts on Transportation

## Themes

- Cutting transportation costs
- Using public transportation

**Background notes:** Transportation is a hidden cost for some people. They don't consider it as much as they should, even when making some important decisions— about whether to take a job, for example. You can use the material presented on this topic to help your students assess the costs of travel and to make choices about it while they also practice language skills related to it. Note that the rate schedule on page 26 presents information and vocabulary with little explanation. Most students who use public transportation will probably have little trouble with it. Others may appreciate a bit of help before they use the rest of that page and page 27.

## Preparation possibilities

- Think about: public transportation available in your area
- Bring to class: rate schedules, maps, and other information about local public transportation

## Technology resources

- Search topic: *public transportation* (by geographic area)
- Web pages to try: BART (Bay Area Rapid Transit in San Francisco, and other specific transportation systems)

## Student pages

- Page 26 includes: a public bus rate schedule, general information on transportation costs, and a challenge story involving relative transportation costs (Note: While student opinion about the challenge activity may vary, the best case can probably be made for using the subway with a monthly pass. It is faster, more certain, and easier to budget for than the new friend's car.)
- Page 27 includes: a word list you may adjust for your class and student activities

**Especially for ESL:** People new to the area and to English may need assistance understanding public transportation systems. Ask: What kind of public transportation did you use in your first country?

## Extra idioms and slang to introduce

- *Leave somebody high and dry:* forget somebody; leave somebody without help
- *Get a free ride:* Get something free (not just a ride)

**Thoughts to share with learners:** Car pools are an excellent way to save money and cut pollution. It pays to spend some time finding just the right one. You need to have a group of people whose driving schedules and locations work well together.

**Questions to ask learners:** Who in the class uses public transportation? What kind? Is it easy to use?

**Projects to assign learners:** Collect and bring to class maps, rate schedules, and other information for local transportation systems. Compare the costs of different systems to see which look most cost-effective for you.

**A fascinating fact to share:** Sir Goldsworthy Gurney of England invented the bus in 1830. The first one was driven by steam and had 18 seats.

# Lesson 9: Thoughts on Transportation

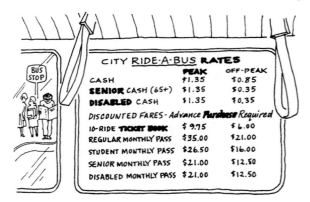

Going places costs money. That sounds simple, but sometimes we forget it. We might say a movie costs just $5. But getting there costs something, too. So the price of the movie is more than $5. When you travel regularly, you need to budget for it. You also need to find the best way to go. Often that means public **transportation**. It costs less than going in your own car. It can be faster, too. And if you aren't driving, you can read or relax when you travel.

$$$$$$$$$$$$$$$$$$$$$$$$$$$$$$$$$$$$$$$$$$$$$$$$$$$$$$$

## Reader Challenge: Getting there

You have a new job, and you are delighted. The work sounds like fun and pays $10 an hour. But the job is in a factory all the way across town. It's five miles from where you live and you don't have a car. How will you get there?

You won't start work for another week. So you try the trip several ways.

The first time you go in style. You **hail a cab**. But you are sorry before the trip ends. You thought it would be fun to see the city. But you watch the **meter** the whole way. The **fare** is $8.50. The ride takes 45 minutes and the driver looks angry when you give him a 50-cent tip.

You take a subway back. It costs just $2. But you have to **transfer** twice, and you get confused. You take an **outbound** train instead of an **inbound**, so your travel time is two hours. But you know you could get a monthly pass for $35 and cut the time to half an hour.

The next day you borrow a bicycle. You ride to the plant in an hour, and you can buy a bicycle for $200. But it rains and snows a lot in your city. How many days could you use it?

That evening at a party you meet somebody new. He works at the factory where your job is. He lives near you, and has a car. He says you can ride with him if you pay him $25 a month and buy half the gas for the trip. He doesn't know how much that will be because he just got the car.

Which choice is most **cost-effective**? That night, you lie in bed wondering.

**Here's your challenge:** What do you decide? Is the job worth having? How will you get there?

## Lesson 9: Thoughts on Transportation

## Word list

| | | | | |
|---|---|---|---|---|
| rate(s) | disabled | transportation | fare(s) | inbound |
| peak | purchase | hail a cab | transfer | cost-effective |
| senior | ticket book | meter | outbound | |

## Increasing your understanding

1. Look at the word list. If you don't know a word, find out what it means. Try to figure it out from the way it is used on page 26. Or look it up in a dictionary.

2. Supply the missing words from the word list:

   (a) At the end of the story on page 26, you wonder which choice is most _____.

   (b) Once you travel to the factory in style. You _____, but later you are sorry.

   (c) The rate schedule on page 26 shows different prices for _____ and off-peak hours.

   (d) Buying a 10-ride _____ is one way to save money.

   (e) People in wheelchairs can get a special _____ monthly pass.

## Questions to discuss

1. How do you answer the challenge on page 26? What will you do? Why?

2. Whose fault is pollution? Is it yours? Should you use public transportation to help clean the air? Should everybody? Anybody?

3. What would happen in your area if everybody always used public transportation? What would change? Brainstorm your answers.

## Things to write about

1. How good is the public transportation in your area? Write a letter to the editor of your newspaper. Say how it should be improved. Or say why you think it is okay the way it is.

2. What's good about traveling by bus? What's not so good? Write your ideas in a paragraph.

## Things to do

1. With a partner, role-play two people from the story on page 26. One of you can be the person with the new job. The other can be the new friend from the party. Talk about getting to work. How much should you pay the friend? What happens if you get sick and don't ride for a few days? What happens if two more people ride with you?

2. How many kinds of public transportation have you used? Make a list. Then decide which one you liked best, and share your ideas with classmates.

3. How can you convince more people to ride the bus? Imagine that you and three or four classmates work for a local bus company. Brainstorm ways to get more riders. Write your ideas down. Then share them with your full class.

4. Do your friends and family members use public transportation? Why do they or don't they? Ask around outside class. Then share what you find with your class.

*Life Skills Literacy:*
*Things to Know About Spending and Saving Money*

# Lesson 10: Money Emergencies

## Themes

- Preparing for financial emergencies
- Saving money

**Background notes:** These pages sound a theme common to most educational material on personal finances: the need to plan and save for emergencies. That's an approach more easily stated than taken, as many of your students may have already discovered. So you might let the student material on page 29 preach about the need while you spend some class time on the how's. Some of the "Thoughts" and "Questions" below will help you start the discussion.

## Preparation possibilities

- Think about: sources of financial emergency assistance in your area (food banks, welfare offices)
- Bring to class: bank pamphlets and account application forms

## Technology resources

- Search topic: *emergency food* (and other specific emergencies); *pawn shops*
- Web pages to try: banks by name, relief organizations (like Canadian Food for the Hungry)

## Student pages

- Page 29 includes: HELP rules for money emergencies; some thoughts about saving, and a dialogue about two friends, one with a financial emergency
- Page 30 includes: a word list you may adjust for your class and student activities

**Especially for ESL:** People new to western culture might need more assistance than others distinguishing between high-cost, "nobody refused"

commercial lenders and banks. Say: Banks are usually the safest, best places to go for loans. Ask: What do people in your home country do when they have financial emergencies?

## Extra idioms and slang to introduce

- *Loan shark:* usurer, person who lends money at very high rates
- *Save somebody's neck:* save somebody from a problem

**Thoughts to share with learners:** Credit unions sometimes offer higher interest on savings and lower-cost loans than regular banks. But credit unions are open only to people in special groups — like the employees of a certain company. And you should always compare rates before deciding on a loan or a savings place. Many people have trouble saving. Some companies will put some of every paycheck into a savings account if you ask them to. This means you never see the money. So you might be less tempted to use it.

**Questions to ask learners:** Are there any easy ways to save money? What does "writing a bad check" mean? (It can mean having an overdraft or "bouncing a check.") Do any companies around here promise to lend money to anybody who wants it? Are they good companies? Is lending money to friends and family members a good idea?

**Projects to assign learners:** Visit local banks and get information about opening accounts and interest rates. Find out about emergency assistance in your area. Share what you learn with the class.

**A fascinating fact to share:** About 20 percent of American families do not have bank accounts.

# Lesson 10: Money Emergencies

## HELP RULES FOR MONEY **EMERGENCIES**

**H**ave money saved for emergencies
**E**xpect emergencies
**L**ook ahead for emergencies
**P**lan for emergencies

Here are four HELP rules for money emergencies. Read them and **compare** them. Are they different? Not really. They all say the same thing. You need to plan for emergencies. You can't know just what they will be. But you do know there will be some. Everybody has emergencies. Cars break down. People get sick. Accidents happen. Suddenly you need more money. So plan ahead and save some money. Then you'll be better off, even in bad emergencies.

$$$$$$$$$$$$$$$$$$$$$$$$$$$$$$$$$$$$$$$$$$$$$$$$$$$$$$$$$$$

## Dialogue: Got any money?

**First Friend:** I have a **financial** emergency.

**Second Friend:** Again? You had one of those last week.

**FF:** I know. My cat got sick. Now my car is sick. Know any good **pawn shops**?

**SF:** You can't have much left to **hock**. You need to make some money.

**FF:** But I don't work at a **mint**.

**SF:** You don't work at all, and you should.

**FF:** But I'm going to school.

**SF:** You won't be if you use all your money on cats and cars.

**FF:** Do you know what the world needs? A financial 911. A phone number for economic emergencies.

**SF:** To send out money when you're broke? Good luck. Anyway, there is a phone number for financial emergencies.

**FF:** Tell me more.

**SF:** It's the number for your bank or **credit union**. You call and get money **transferred** from your savings account to your **checking account**. Then you have

the money you need. You can **access** it with a check or a **debit card**.

**FF:** But I don't have a savings account. Or a bank, for that matter. Or a debit card. Just a credit card. I had a checking account but I kept **overdrawing** so the bank closed it.

**SF:** Then the first thing you need is a job. The second thing is a savings account. Put your money in that and earn interest. You can go to school and make money, too. And you'll have savings for emergencies.

**FF:** But I can't save money. I already owe seven thousand bucks.

**SF:** Uh-oh. Then forget the job and bank. The first think to look for is a good financial **adviser**.

**FF:** That's the first thing to look for after money. Got any of that to lend?

**SF:** No!

*Life Skills Literacy:*
*Things to Know About Spending and Saving Money*

Name_____ Date _____

## Lesson10: Money Emergencies

### Word list

| | | | | |
|---|---|---|---|---|
| emergencies | pawn shop(s) | credit union | checking | debit card |
| compare | hock | transfer(red) | account | overdraw(ing) |
| financial | mint | | access | adviser |

### Increasing your understanding

1. Look at the word list. If you don't know a word, find out what it means. Try to figure it out from the way it is used on page 29. Or look it up in a dictionary.

2. Supply the missing words from the word list:

   (a) In the story on page 29, the first friend has a _____ emergency.

   (b) If you call your bank, you can get money _____ from one account to another.

   (c) The first friend had a checking account, but kept _____ it, so the bank closed it.

   (d) "You can't have much left to _____," says the second friend.

   (e) You can access money from a checking account with a check or a _____.

### Questions to discuss

1. Would you lend money to somebody like the first friend in the story? Why or why not?

2. How much do you need to save? Some experts say working people should have savings equal to what they can earn in six months. What do you think about this? Can most people do it?

3. Some people say "it takes money to make money." What does that mean? Is it true? Why or why not?

### Things to write about

1. What can you do if you have a financial emergency and you are broke? Write a paragraph about your ideas.

2. Write a slogan for a bank that wants people to save some money every month. The slogan should give at least one good reason for saving money.

### Things to do

1. With a partner, role-play the story on page 29. See if the first friend can convince the second to lend some money.

2. What kinds of financial emergencies can happen? List at least five emergencies that happen to a lot of people. Put them in order starting with the most serious.

3. Make a poster showing the HELP rules on page 29. Change the wording if you want.

4. Where's the best place to put your savings? Outside of class, ask five or six friends what they think. Is one bank or credit union in your area better than the others? Why? Share what you learn with your class.

*Life Skills Literacy:*
*Things to Know About Spending and Saving Money*

# Lesson 11: About Insurance

## Theme

- Getting insurance in reasonable amounts

**Background notes:** Insurance is a mystery to many inexperienced consumers. They know they are supposed to have some of it, but they are not sure just what. And they know that paying for it is as much fun as buying a water heater. It won't bring much immediate pleasure. But it will take a chunk of money; in 1995, Americans spent $3,621 per person just for health insurance. Their national health care system gave Canadians a better break, but they too had other forms of insurance to buy. What coverage is sensible and what is not? Who should buy what? There are no easy answers. These pages are designed to help your students understand that insurance needs vary greatly from one individual to the next. Only they, with the help of agents and other resources, can determine what is right for them.

## Preparation possibilities

- Think about: the apparent insurance needs of your students
- Bring to class: pamphlets and other information about insurance of various types

## Technology resources

- Search topic: *insurance; insurance regulations*
- Web pages to try: Insurance Information Institute, National Insurance Consumer Helpline

## Student pages

- Page 32 includes: a message displayed by the Insurance Information Institute on the Internet, a basic introduction to insurance needs, and a story about a woman who is over-insured. Note that the I.I.I. message has a relatively high readability level, so students may need assistance with it.
- Page 33 includes: a word list you may adjust for your class and student activities

**Especially for ESL:** The concept of health and some other forms of insurance may be new to some ESL students. Ask: How did you pay for health care in your countries? What insurance did most people have?

## Extra idioms and slang to introduce

- *Pay up:* pay, settle accounts
- *Pay the piper:* take the consequences; pay for what you did

**Thoughts to share with learners:** How much life insurance you need depends in part on how many people depend on you. Your "dependents" are people you support with money. Your "beneficiaries" are people who get your money when you die.

**Questions to ask learners:** What's the most important insurance? What should you get first if you can't get everything you would like? What happens to people in the United States who have no health insurance but get ill? (Some get poor treatment or no treatment, and some build up enormous bills.)

**Projects to assign learners:** Find out about health insurance offered by major local employers. Ask friends who work there. Or call personnel offices and ask.

**A fascinating fact to share:** Lloyd's of London was a famous insurance company that once insured Jimmy Durante's nose and Liberace's fingers.

# Lesson 11: About Insurance

WELCOME to the **Insurance** Information **Institute** (I.I.I.) Consumer **Web Site**. I.I.I. is a nonprofit, educational and **communications** organization **sponsored** by the auto, home, and business insurance industry. I.I.I is **dedicated** to educating consumers about what insurance is and how it works.

How much insurance do you need? Agents say "it all depends." It depends on who you are. It depends on how old you are. It depends on what you own. It depends on who is in your family. How can you decide what to get? The I.I.I. might be able to help. That organization gives free information to consumers. If you look it up on a **computer**, you see a message like the one at the left.

$$$$$$$$$$$$$$$$$$$$$$$$$$$$$$$$$$$$$$$$$$$$$$$$$$$$$$$$$$$$$$$$

## Story: How much is too much?

Judith Ivers thought insurance was a good thing. She insured everything she had.

She had a good **health plan** through her job. If she got sick, the plan would pay for everything. She also had the best car insurance she could find. It cost almost as much as her car did.

She carried wonderful home insurance. If her house burned, the plan would pay. If somebody got hurt in Judith's house, the plan would pay a lot.

She had a huge life insurance policy. If she died, the money would go to her cousin. Judith didn't know the cousin, but she didn't care. She knew insurance was a good thing.

She insured her jewels, too. If anybody stole them, she would get her money back. Then came the cat and dog. Judith got health insurance for them, too. She knew **veterinarians** can cost a lot of money.

"Now I can go away and everything will be safe," she said. And she planned a vacation. She got plane tickets and air travel insurance. She **reserved** a rental car with a lot of insurance. She even bought rain insurance. If it rained on her vacation, she would get some money to make up for it.

But the day before her trip, Judith felt sick. "I'm glad I have good insurance," she said. Then she called her doctor.

"I see what's wrong," the doctor said. "You need to eat more."

"But I can't afford to," said Judith. "I have spent all my money on my trip and my insurance."

"Well at least you aren't sick," said the doctor. "You're just insurance poor. So I'm going to send you to a **specialist**. He's my insurance **consultant**. If you see him today, you can still take your trip."

*Life Skills Literacy:*
*Things to Know About Spending and Saving Money*

## Lesson 11: About Insurance

### Word list

| | | | | |
|---|---|---|---|---|
| insurance | communica- | dedicat(ed) | veterinarian(s) | consultant |
| institute | tion(s) | computer | reserve(d) | |
| Web site | sponsor(ed) | health plan | specialist | |

### Increasing your understanding

1. Look at the word list. If you don't know a word, find out what it means. Try to figure it out from the way it is used on page 32. Or look it up in a dictionary.

2. Supply the missing words from the word list:

   (a) The information in the box on page 32 is from the I.I.I. Consumer _____.

   (b) I.I.I. is _____ to educating consumers about what insurance is.

   (c) The story says Judith Ivers had a good _____ in case she got sick.

   (d) For her vacation, Judith _____ a rental car.

   (e) "I'm going to send you to a _____," the doctor said. "He's my insurance _____."

### Questions to discuss

1. What kind of woman is the person in the story on page 32. Do you think you would like Judith Ivers? Why or why not?

2. How can you decide how much insurance to get? Read the paragraph at the top of page 32 again. Then brainstorm some more ideas.

3. Is buying insurance like betting? Which is the better way to spend your money?

### Things to write about

1. What don't you want to insure? Write a paragraph about something you like but that you won't insure. Maybe it's not worth much money. Maybe there's some other reason.

2. Can you get a better price? Imagine that you have a home insurance policy from Acme Insurance. Now you have found another good policy that costs less. Write a letter asking Acme to lower its price. Tell them what you will do if the price does not change.

### Things to do

1. With a partner, role-play the story on page 32. One of you can be Judith Ivers. The other can be her doctor. Use your own names if you want. Decide what you think the specialist will say.

2. How much life insurance do you need? Make a list of at least five facts about you that an insurance agent might ask. One of them can be your age.

3. How much will you pay? Imagine that you have a new camera worth $1,200. You think it will last 10 years. You will insure it if you can get a policy at a good price. Decide how much you are willing to pay every year. Compare your answer to your classmates' ideas.

4. What's in the yellow pages? Outside of class, look in a phone book under "insurance." What did you learn? Share what you find with your classmates.

*Life Skills Literacy:*
*Things to Know About Spending and Saving Money*

# Lesson 12: Discretionary Income

## Themes

- Where nondiscretionary income goes
- Money we can spend as we want

**Background notes:** People new to the work force are typically distressed to learn that not all their money goes into their own pockets. These pages give an opportunity to consider the topic from two directions. The first is where money that never reaches our pockets goes—for taxes and insurance, for example. The second is how we should and how we do handle our discretionary funds. Both approaches relate to many other subjects in this set of *Things to Know*, such as budgeting and identifying essential expenses. You might wish to help students make connections with earlier activities and discussions.

## Preparation possibilities

- Think about: the apparent discretionary spending patterns of your students
- Bring to class: pamphlets and other information about taxation and other deductions; a typical payroll slip showing deductions made by a local business

## Technology resources

- Search topic: *discretionary income*
- Web pages to try: TGE Demographics; Resources for Economists on the Internet

## Student pages

- Page 35 includes: definitions of *disposable income* and *discretionary income*; an introduction to the idea of disposable income; and a challenge activity about using disposable income
- Page 36 includes: a word list you may adjust for your class and student activities

**Especially for ESL:** People new to the United States and Canada may need additional assistance understanding where nondisposable income goes. Ask: In your home countries, do workers have a lot of deductions made from their pay? What are they?

## Extra idioms and slang to introduce

- *Take-home pay:* the amount of money that actually goes home with a worker
- *Fun money:* discretionary money you can spend for anything

**Thoughts to share with learners:** When you take a job, ask how much money you expect in your paycheck. Most people agree that food and clothing are essentials. But that doesn't mean that all the food you buy and all the clothing you buy fit that category. Snacks at the movies and funny hats are not essentials.

**Questions to ask learners:** Are deductions for things like taxes a good idea? What would happen if everybody got all their pay, then wrote checks for taxes and insurance? Would that be better? What could you do if you work for a big company and think it is taking too much money out of your pay?

**Projects to assign learners:** Look at one of your own paychecks. Make a list of the items deducted from your pay and bring it to class to share. Ask friends and family members if they have the same deductions.

**A fascinating fact to share:** Two thirds of all American households had some disposable income in 1994. One third had nothing left after paying for things like taxes and essential items.

# Lesson 12: Discretionary Income

## Disposable Income
— the income left for a person after taxes are deducted

## Discretionary Income
— the part of a person's income that does not go for essentials like housing and food.

Is your money yours? Some of it is, and some of it isn't. Some of your income probably goes for taxes. You get what's left. But some of that goes for **benefits** like insurance and essentials like food. What's left over is your discretionary income. Is it sometimes hard to decide what to do with it? Don't worry. Lots of people are ready to help. Every day a thousand **advertisers** will tell you what to buy. They want you to spend it on whatever they are selling. How do you spend your extra money?

$ $ $ $ $ $ $ $ $ $ $ $ $ $ $ $ $ $ $ $ $ $ $ $ $ $ $ $ $ $ $ $ $ $ $ $ $ $ $ $ $ $ $ $ $ $ $ $

## Reader Challenge: The Nightmare

You are studying **economics**. One class is about disposable income and discretionary income. "People use discretionary income lots of different ways," the teacher says. "Some get **luxuries** and some just throw it away on little things. Some people are **sensible** and save a lot. Still others **invest** it. That's a really good idea."

Later you tell your roommates about the class. "I'm going to think about my disposable money," you say. "Maybe I'm wasting a lot. And if I get that raise at work Monday, I'll have more money to think about."

You know you shouldn't plan on the raise. But you think you will get it. If you do, you will buy the new **boom box** you want. You are happy when you go to bed that night. But then you have a **nightmare**. In the dream, you hear your roommates laughing in the kitchen. You go to see what they are doing. They are ripping up dollar bills and stuffing them into the trash.

"Stop!" you yell. But they don't. They laugh.

"We're getting rid of your raise for you," says one.

When you wake up you are glad the story was a dream. You tell your roommates about it and they really laugh.

That day is Saturday, and you go shopping. You think you will just get soap and other **incidentals**. Then you stop at the music store just to look at the boom box you might get. You find out that it's on sale!

"If I get my raise, I'll get this box Monday night," you tell the salesman.

"But the sale ends today," the salesman says. "The price goes up 30 dollars on Monday."

"Oh no," you say. "This is a real nightmare."

**Here's your challenge:** Do you get the box now?

*Life Skills Literacy:*
*Things to Know About Spending and Saving Money*

# Lesson 12: Discretionary Income

## Word list

| | | | |
|---|---|---|---|
| disposable | benefit(s) | luxuries | boom box |
| deduct(ed) | advertiser(s) | sensible | nightmare |
| discretionary | economics | invest | incidental(s) |

## Increasing your understanding

1. Look at the word list. If you don't know a word, find out what it means. Try to figure it out from the way it is used on page 35. Or look it up in a dictionary.

2. Supply the missing words from the word list:

   (a) In the story on page 35, you are studying _____.

   (b) One class is about disposable income and _____ income.

   (c) Soap and other _____ are what you expect to buy.

   (d) A thousand _____ tell you what to buy, says the paragraph at the top of page 35.

   (e) Some of your income might go for _____ like insurance.

## Questions to discuss

1. How do you answer the challenge on page 35? Do you buy the box now or wait?
2. What do people have deducted from their paychecks? One thing is taxes. Brainstorm some others.
3. Do most people spend their discretionary income wisely? Give reasons for your answer.

## Things to write about

1. What should you do if you really want to buy something and can't afford it? Write your answer in a paragraph or two.
2. Can you get a raise? Imagine that you sell shoes in a store. Ask your boss for a raise. Say why you should get it and why you need it.

## Things to do

1. With a partner, role-play the parts of two roommates from the story on page 35. Imagine that they can't pay the rent. They have spent too much money on things like boom boxes. What will they do now?
2. Draw a picture for the story on page 35. It might show people or an apartment or a boom box.
3. What do you want to buy with your discretionary income? Make a list of six things you would like to have. Underline the two that are most important to you. Will any of them help you make more money? Underline those twice.
4. How many ads do you hear and see in a day? Outside of class, try to count them for a day. Then talk with your class about what you find out.

*Life Skills Literacy:*
*Things to Know About Spending and Saving Money*

# Lesson 13: Sales Promotions

## Themes

- Taking advantage of sales and other promotions
- Understanding the merchant's side of sales and other promotions

**Background notes:** All the world loves a sale. But all the world should also be careful of sales. Some are real and good, some are not. It may seem great to find an electric mixer for 25 percent off the usual price. But it's not so helpful if the original price was 30 percent more than another dealer would have charged. Using these pages should help your students understand that careful shoppers win at sales, but that careless shoppers lose.

## Preparation possibilities

- Think about: the sales behavior of retailers in your area
- Bring to class: newspaper ads and other promotional materials that will help learners apply the material in these pages to their own marketplace

## Technology resources

- Search topic: *furniture* (or other retail items, for an interesting glance at the industry)
- Web pages to try: Western Home Furnishing Association (for advice to retailers trying to increase profits)

## Student pages

- Page 38 includes: an introduction to sales and other promotions; a dialogue between two people seeking to improve sales at their furniture store
- Page 39 includes: a word list you may adjust for your class and student activities

**Especially for ESL:** The suggested use of a calendar in Activity 2 under "Things to Do" on page 39 offers an opportunity for conveying cultural information to ESL students. You might wish to spend some time helping them to see how the marketing calendar connects with events like religious and national holidays. Ask: Could you plan on annual sales in your native country?

## Extra idioms and slang to introduce

- *Street-wise:* knowledgeable about practical things
- *Too good to be true:* unbelievable

**Thoughts to share with learners:** If you want to buy a sales item, it is okay for the salesperson to suggest something more expensive. But it is not okay for the salesperson to refuse to sell the cheaper item or to talk about how bad it is. That is bait and switch, which is illegal. You should report it to a local consumer protection agency (like the state attorney general's office). It is often best to shop at stores where people think you might shop again. Their owners and clerks are likely to try and satisfy you.

**Questions to ask learners:** Do you know any stores that offer really good sales in this area? Have you ever seen stores using bait and switch or other bad sales practices?

**Projects to assign learners:** Attend a special sale at a local store. Look around and decide if the store has good deals. Share what you find with your classmates.

**A fascinating fact to share:** In 1938, the Wheeler-Lea Amendment made false advertising illegal in the United States.

# Lesson 13: Sales Promotions

Do you take advantage of sales and other **promotions**? Watch the ads and you can, but don't be fooled. Make sure prices are really low before you buy. If they aren't, go somewhere else. When you shop, think about the store owners. What are they trying to do? They are trying to make a profit. They want to get as much from you as they can. Some use low prices to do that. But others don't. It's up to you to decide which is which.

## Dialogue: A new approach

**Store Owner:** We've got to sell more furniture. Let's get a new sales **gimmick**. What should it be?

**Store Clerk:** I don't know, boss. The same old stuff isn't working. Nobody pays attention to our "Going Out of Business" sign anymore.

**SO:** You're right. And we had three "Special **Clearances**" last year, plus a "Pre-Christmas Sale." The year before we had a "New Year's **Giveaway**," a "President's Birthday **Bonanza**," and a "May **Markdown**." None of them worked.

**SC:** The "Giveaway" was the worst. People got mad when we gave them cheap candy. Then we advertised "**Discontinued Merchandise**." But we didn't have any. So we offered people something else. Then they **accused** us of **bait and switch**.

**SO:** How about a "Grand Opening?"

**SC:** But we've been open for 20 years. We'd have to close and remodel, then reopen.

**SO:** Too expensive. We could send out a mailing with special prices for our old customers. We could call it a "**Preferred** Customer Discount."

**SC:** But we need new customers. Besides, I have a different idea.

**SO:** It better be good, or we'll be closing for good.

**SC:** Let's do what the **competition** does. Let's really lower our prices for once.

**SO:** You mean sell things cheaper?

**SC:** Sure. That's what the discount houses do.

**SO:** But where would our profit go?

**SC:** What profit? We aren't selling enough to make a profit. If we cut out ads that don't work, we'll save money. Let's put up one new sign that says "Honest **Value** All the Time." This time we'll mean it. Then we'll get our business back.

**SO:** Are you sure?

**SC:** Yes. Honest value always works.

**SO:** We'll try it. If sales go up, you get a big raise. If not, you're out of a job. So am I.

**SC:** I think I'll start right now.

© 1998 J. Weston Walch, Publisher

38

*Life Skills Literacy:*
*Things to Know About Spending and Saving Money*

Name_____ Date _____

## Lesson 13: Sales Promotions

## Word list

| | | | | |
|---|---|---|---|---|
| promotion(s) | giveaway | discontinue(d) | bait and switch | value |
| gimmick | bonanza | merchandise | prefer(red) | |
| clearance(s) | markdown | accuse(d) | competition | |

## Increasing your understanding

1. Look at the word list. If you don't know a word, find out what it means. Try to figure it out from the way it is used on page 38. Or look it up in a dictionary.

2. Supply the missing words from the word list:

   (a) The boss in the story on page 38 wants a new sales _____.

   (b) "Let's do what the _____ does," the clerk suggests.

   (c) The store advertised one thing and tried to sell another. Customers _____ it of bait and switch.

   (d) The boss suggests a mailing about a _____ Customer Discount.

   (e) The paragraph at the top of page 38 talks about sales and other _____.

## Questions to discuss

1. Will the boss in the story really offer honest value? Give reasons for your answers.

2. What bad gimmicks do stores use? The story talks about "bait and switch." What is that? What other sales tricks do you need to watch for? Brainstorm your answers.

3. Why don't some stores have sales? Are the regular prices too high in stores that do have sales?

## Things to write about

1. What if you owned a pet store? Imagine that you pay $100 for a puppy. How much will you sell it for? Why? Write a paragraph giving your answers.

2. What can you do if a store uses bait and switch? You can complain. Imagine that Fun Phones advertises a cheap telephone. But when you ask for one, the clerk says they are all gone. He tries to sell you an expensive phone instead. Write a letter complaining to the manager.

## Things to do

1. Act out the dialogue on page 38 with a partner. Decide if you think the new plan will work.

2. Make a buying calendar for the year. Write down two good things to buy in each month. For example, you might buy Christmas cards in January, when they are cheap.

3. With three or four classmates, make a musical radio ad for a furniture sale. Use "Sara's Sofas" for the store name if you want. Or make up your own. Write words for the ad. Then sing them or say them with some sound effects.

4. How many sales can you find? Outside of class, see how many sales you can find around you. Which ones look good? Share what you find in class.

*Life Skills Literacy:*
*Things to Know About Spending and Saving Money*

# Lesson 14: Spending at Home

**Themes**

- Shopping by catalog, phone, and electronic equipment
- Watching for mail and phone fraud

**Background notes:** Direct mail, phone, and electronic approaches to consumers have been growing at a startling pace ever since Aaron Montgomery Ward sent out his first catalog in 1872. And recent Internet growth suggests that the pace will continue to accelerate. This is good news and bad for consumers; mail, phone lines, and electronic distribution systems are convenient not just for customers and providers, but for criminals, too. Today, one can shop at home, work at home, and steal at home, all with singular ease. These pages will help you alert your students to both the advantages and dangers of buying without seeing actual merchandise.

**Preparation possibilities**

- Think about: direct marketers and consumer protection agencies in your area
- Bring to class: sample catalogs; news stories about direct marketing and problems

**Technology resources**

- Search topic: *telemarketing, anti-telemarketing, direct mail*
- Web pages to try: Mr. Postman and Private Citizens (for material on avoiding telemarketing and mail sales campaigns); Better Business Bureau

**Student pages**

- Page 41 includes: an introduction to shopping at home; a story about a job helping to police direct marketers

- Page 42 includes: a word list you may adjust for your class and student activities

**Especially for ESL:** People with limited English skills are particularly vulnerable to fast-talking telemarketers. Say: If you don't fully understand the call, end it. Ask: Are direct mail and telemarketing common in your home country?

**Extra idioms and slang to introduce**

- *Junk mail:* unsolicited and undesirable mail
- *Pigeon:* fraud victim

**Thoughts to share with learners:** Don't participate in chain letters or sweepstakes and prize promotions that ask for money. If a deal sounds too good to be true, it probably is.

**Questions to ask learners:** Have you had someone take advantage of you on the telephone? Do you want to tell the class about it? What do you see are the advantages of shopping at home? The disadvantages?

**Projects to assign learners:** Call the Better Business Bureau. Ask for a report on a local business that interests you (generally done by leaving a recorded phone message). Visit a local consumer protection agency and ask for pamphlets helpful to consumers.

**A fascinating fact to share:** In 1993, American consumers made 22,000 complaints to Better Business Bureau offices about mail and phone solicitations.

# Lesson 14: Spending at Home

Many people work at home these days. Many people spend money at home, too. Doing that is easy. You can fill your house with **catalogs**. A **telemarketer** might call. Or you can use a computer. You can order everything from books to cars over the **Internet**. Shopping at home has some **advantages**. But it also has some dangers. You might get **bargains** shopping at home. But you might get taken. So be careful, and don't take chances.

$ $ $ $ $ $ $ $ $ $ $ $ $ $ $ $ $ $ $ $ $ $ $ $ $ $ $ $ $ $ $ $ $ $ $ $ $ $ $ $ $ $ $ $ $ $ $ $

## Story: The perfect job

"Ask for what you want," Diketa's father told her. "You may not get it. But you won't know until you ask."

"Here's what I want," said Diketa. "I want a job. I want a job staying home and watching TV and reading and talking on the phone. That's what I like to do. So I want to get paid for it."

"You probably can't do that," said her father. "But it can't hurt to ask. Go ahead and try."

Diketa went to an **employment agency**. A woman asked what kind of job Diketa wanted. Diketa told her, and the woman smiled. "I have just the job for you," she said.

The job was with a consumer protection agency. It wanted somebody like Diketa to read **mail order** catalogs and answer telemarketer calls. She could also watch the sales channel on TV. She would be looking for misleading ads and signs of **fraud**.

"There are good mail order houses and telemarketers," the woman said. "They work hard for sales and customer **loyalty**. But some criminals use the mail and phone for fraud. They run **scams**. They cheat people. They get people's money and give nothing back."

"What would I do if I found things like that?" Diketa asked.

"You would tell your agency. And it would report to the **Better Business Bureau** and the **Federal Trade Commission**. It would also complain to the state's **attorney general**. The government could put the crooks out of business and maybe even arrest them."

"Great," said Diketa. "I want the job."

She told her father about it that night. "Amazing," he said.

"I followed your advice," Diketa said. "I asked for what I wanted. And I got it. You are a wise man."

"No," her father said. "You are a very lucky young woman."

*Life Skills Literacy:*
*Things to Know About Spending and Saving Money*

## Lesson 14: Spending at Home

**$ ACTIVITY PAGE**

### Word list

| | | | |
|---|---|---|---|
| catalog(s) | bargain(s) | fraud | Bureau |
| telemarketer | employment | loyalty | Federal Trade |
| Internet | agency | scam(s) | Commission |
| advantage(s) | mail order | Better Business | attorney general |

### Increasing your understanding

1. Look at the word list. If you don't know a word, find out what it means. Try to figure it out from the way it is used on page 41. Or look it up in a dictionary.

2. Supply the missing words from the word list:

   (a) Shopping at home has some _____, according to the paragraph at the top of page 41.

   (b) You can get _____ shopping at home, but you can also get taken.

   (c) In the story on page 41, Diketa went to an _____ _____ to look for a job.

   (d) In her new job she will look for misleading ads and signs of _____.

   (e) Diketa's agency might tell the Better Business Bureau, the Federal Trade Commission, and the state's _____ about things like fraud.

### Questions to discuss

1. Will Diketa like the job she gets in the story on page 41? Why do you answer the way you do?

2. Who suffers most from telemarketing fraud? What kind of people are most likely to be hurt? What about good companies? Do they get hurt?

3. What will the world be like in 50 years? Will there be any stores? How will we shop? Will we get better bargains that way? Brainstorm your answers.

### Things to write about

1. What can you say? Imagine that you get a lot of telemarketing calls you don't want. What should you say? Write a good answer you can use.

2. Do you like shopping by mail? Write a paragraph saying why or why not.

### Things to do

1. Role-play the parts of Diketa and the woman at the employment agency in the story on page 41. Use your own names if you want. See if you can think of another job Diketa might like.

2. How can you build customer loyalty? Imagine that you and three or four classmates all work for a mail order clothing catalog. Get together and make up four or five rules for keeping customers happy. One of them might be: "Fill every order the day it arrives."

3. Could you be on the sales channel? Imagine that you have a job selling something on TV. Use a watch or a book or something else close by. Show your classmates how you would get customers to call and order it.

42

*Life Skills Literacy:*
*Things to Know About Spending and Saving Money*

# Lesson 15: Free Entertainment

## Themes

- Finding free and inexpensive entertainment
- Financial self-discipline

## Background notes:

The typical American family devotes $1,500 a year to entertainment. But some families and individuals don't have the funds to spend at that level. What can they do without skipping entertainment entirely? Find free and inexpensive options, of course. That might sound obvious, yet a lot of possibilities are ignored. Professional football stadiums fill with tens of thousands of people paying high prices, while fine athletes in minor sports and amateur leagues perform before empty bleachers. These pages will help you lead your students to consider possibilities open to them in their own areas.

## Preparation possibilities

- Think about: inexpensive entertainment possibilities in your area
- Bring to class: fliers and other information about local entertainment resources and facilities

## Technology resources

- Search topic: *entertainment, free entertainment, recreation* (all narrowed by location and type)
- Web pages to try: Free Forum (and many others, using the Web as inexpensive entertainment)

## Student pages

- Page 44 includes: a poster about a symphony orchestra; a brief introduction to free and low-cost entertainment; a challenge activity about inexpensive entertainment

- Page 45 includes: a word list you may adjust for your class and student activities

## Especially for ESL:

People new to your area may need more help than others finding inexpensive entertainment. Ask: Could you find free entertainment in your native country?

## Extra idioms and slang to introduce

- *Freebie:* anything free
- *Gate crasher:* somebody who goes to an event without an invitation or ticket

## Thoughts to share with learners:

*Entertainment* often involves seeing or hearing something done by somebody else—at a concert, for example. *Recreation* often involves doing something yourself—like hiking in a park. Sometimes you can enjoy entertainment free by working at it. You could volunteer to usher at a play. Or you could sell food in the stands at a ball game.

## Questions to ask learners:

Which is better for you? Entertainment or recreation? Are you aware of any low-cost possibilities in this area that others might not know about? Is the Internet a good form of inexpensive recreation? Can you use it free in school? At a local library?

## Projects to assign learners:

Choose a form of entertainment you like. Then find out about the possibilities in this area. Can you find free or inexpensive shows? Do any organizations offer special prices for students? Share what you find with the class.

## A fascinating fact to share:

On July 5, 1986, 800,000 people attended a free concert given by the New York Philharmonic in New York City's Central Park.

# Lesson 15: Free Entertainment

Do you have no-expense days? Days when you spend no money? If not, **schedule** some. Eat leftovers. Find some free **entertainment**. Walk or bicycle, don't ride. If it costs money, skip it. Or trade for it. You can save money doing this. And you will learn something. You will see where your money usually goes. And you will learn some **self-discipline**. You need that to use money wisely.

$$$$$$$$$$$$$$$$$$$$$$$$$$$$$$$$$$$$$$$$$$$$$$$$$$$$$$$$$$$$$

## Reader Challenge: Something for nothing

Your friend Laurent is excited. "Can I borrow five dollars?" he asks.

You don't like lending money to friends. But you can trust Laurent. "I guess so," you tell him. "What's up?"

"I'm going to bet on tomorrow's football game."

"I didn't think you cared about football," you answer.

"I don't," he says. "But I need money fast."

"**Gambling** is not a good way to get it," you say. "And why the hurry?"

"I'm in love," he says.

"Again?" you ask. Laurent falls in love with somebody new at least once a month. "Who is it this time?"

"Sheila," he says. "And we want to go out."

"Why don't each of you pay your own way?"

"We already talked about that. Between us we have 77 cents."

"Then here's a really **radical** idea," you tell him. "Do something free."

"But I want to impress Sheila. She's into **culture**, not bumming around."

"Bumming around? I call it being sensible.

Come over tonight and we'll talk."

When Laurent gets to your place, you pull out a newspaper and a phone book. You begin with the entertainment section of the paper. You find that the **art museum** offers free admission every Friday night. Your symphony orchestra has an open rehearsal on Monday afternoon. And two schools list plays for very low prices.

Then you go to the sports section. "Try school games and **amateur leagues**," you say. "They can be just as much fun as **professional** teams."

Laurent is looking happy.

"Now use the phone book," you say. "Call around and see what else you can find. Then call Sheila and make a free date."

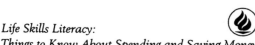

"Okay," he says. "And if you think of anything else, let me know."

**Here's your challenge:** List some free or inexpensive entertainment in your own area.

44

*Life Skills Literacy:*
*Things to Know About Spending and Saving Money*

Name_____ Date _____

## Lesson 15: Free Entertainment

$ ACTIVITY PAGE

## Word list

| | | | |
|---|---|---|---|
| symphony | program(s) | gambling | amateur league(s) |
| orchestra | schedule | radical | professional |
| concert(s) | entertainment | culture | |
| open rehearsal(s) | self-discipline | art museum | |

## Increasing your understanding

1. Look at the word list. If you don't know a word, find out what it means. Try to figure it out from the way it is used on page 44. Or look it up in a dictionary.

2. Supply the missing words from the word list:

(a) "Try school games and _____," you say in the story on page 44.

(b) Sheila is a first-class girl, according to Laurent. She is into _____, he says.

(c) You think Laurent should do something free. "Here's a really _____ idea," you say.

(d) The poster at the top of page 44 says there are _____ every Monday afternoon.

(e) The list at the bottom tells what _____ the orchestra will do.

---

## Questions to discuss

1. How did you answer the challenge on page 44? How many free or inexpensive forms of entertainment can your class think of in five minutes? Brainstorm your answers.

2. What's your favorite low-cost entertainment? Do others in the class share your interest?

3. How do you get self-discipline? Imagine that you know somebody who is a spendthrift. He or she wastes a lot of money. "I just can't help it," the person says. "Money burns a hole in my pocket." What can you tell the person?

## Things to write about

1. If you don't have self-discipline about spending money, what can happen? Write a paragraph giving your answer.

2. Why should tickets cost so much? You want to go to a concert by your favorite group. But tickets cost $42 each. That is too much for you. Write a letter to the manager of the All-Star Theater saying that prices should be lower.

## Things to do

1. Role-play the story on page 44 with a partner. Use different names if you want. Decide what you think Sheila will say when Laurent calls.

2. What are some good reasons for having no-expense days? Talk with three or four classmates about this. Share your ideas with the class.

3. Make a poster telling people that the City Art Museum is open free on Friday nights. Imagine that the museum has paintings by Vincent Van Gogh, a famous artist.

4. Go to any kind of free entertainment. Then tell your class about it.

45

*Life Skills Literacy:*
*Things to Know About Spending and Saving Money*

# Lesson 16: Renting This and Buying That

## Themes

- When renting makes sense
- Reading the small print

**Background notes:** In many large cities today, consumers can rent many of the non-consumables required for daily life, from furniture to cars and from videotapes to some types of clothing. And the rental industry is enormous; America's video rental services together are a $15 billion industry. But renting isn't always the best way to go. While renting a tuxedo for one-time use is a good idea, renting furniture for home use generally is very expensive and therefore a bad idea. These pages will help learners decide when to rent and when to buy, and will expose them to the sometimes difficult language of rental contracts and other consumer documents.

## Preparation possibilities

- Think about: rental businesses in your area
- Bring to class: typical rental agreements from local businesses

## Technology resources

- Search topic: *rental industry*
- Web pages to try: American Rental Association, Rental Association of Canada

## Student pages

- Page 47 includes: a general clause from a typical rental agreement, an introduction to renting, and a dialogue between a reporter and the owner of a new rental agency. Note that the rental clause, based on one used by a real tool-rental company, has a reading level of grade 16, so it may require extra classroom attention. (See also the discussion suggestions in on this page and page 48.)

- Page 48 includes: a word list you may adjust for your class and student activities

**Especially for ESL:** Ask: What things do a lot of people rent in your native country?

## Extra idioms and slang to introduce

- *Fork out/over:* pay
- *Tell it like it is:* speak an unpleasant truth

**Thoughts to share with learners:** Many businesses use complicated contracts and agreements. Be sure you understand them before you sign. Be especially careful if you don't know the reputation of the person or business you are dealing with.

**Questions to ask learners:** What are some things you have rented? Did you get good deals? Do you always read the small print in agreements you sign? Should you? What can you do if you don't understand a contract? When does it make sense to rent a car? What are some things you might buy with friends and then share? What if some friends want to buy and share a sailboat? Is that a good idea?

**Projects to assign learners:** Visit some local rental places. Ask for sample agreements to share with the class. Check the cost of renting videotapes in your area. Who gives the best deal? Do classmates agree?

**A fascinating fact to share:** The international textile industry rents such things as linens for hospitals and uniforms for industry. It did more than $8 billion in business in 1997.

# Lesson 16: Renting This and Buying That

Should you rent it or buy it? That depends on what it is. Is it a videotape you are going to watch just once? Then you should probably rent it. Is it a dining room set you are going to use every day? Then you should probably buy it. And if it's something expensive you don't really need, maybe you should just forget it. But if you rent it, be sure you are getting a good deal. Read the agreement carefully. Is it hard to understand like the one in the box? Then get the renter or somebody else to explain it.

$$$$$$$$$$$$$$$$$$$$$$$$$$$$$$$$$$$$$$$$$$$$$$$$$$$$$$$$$$$$$$$$$$$$

## Dialogue: A friendly business

**Business Person:** Welcome to Friendly Rentals.

**Reporter:** Thanks. I want to write a story on your new business. Why the name?

**BP:** Because everything about us is friendly. We're even going to have friendly contracts. They'll be simple and easy to understand.

**R:** When are you going to open?

**BP:** As soon as the puppies are old enough to rent out.

**R:** Puppies? You're going to rent dogs?

**BP:** Yes. For people who want them but can't afford them. And people who don't have time for them. Good idea, right?

**R:** I'm not sure. Why not videos?

**BP:** There are too many video rental stores in this town already.

**R:** Then rent-to-own furniture. Or tools for the **handy** homeowner.

**BP:** I don't know anything about tools. I'm not very handy myself. And rent-to-own furniture is a bad deal for most customers. They wind up paying much too much for it.

**R:** Clothes, then. **Formal** clothes.

**BP:** Nope. I hate cleaning clothes.

**R:** Then something else. Almost anything **nonconsumable** will do.

**BP:** You're right about that. You shouldn't rent out something consumable like ice cream. It wouldn't come back. But why not dogs? What's the matter with them?

**R:** I'm scared of them. And they bark a lot.

**BP:** Fortunately, most people do like dogs. And dogs are friendly, like the people at Friendly Rentals.

**R:** But what if nobody wants to rent them?

**BP:** Then the dogs will lie around here and lick our faces. Videotapes won't do that. Furniture won't, either. But I guess we won't do much business with you.

**R:** That all depends.

**BP:** On what?

**R:** On whether you add cats to your line. I like cats. I might rent a cat for a weekend.

**BP:** Hey! Now there's a great idea!

*Life Skills Literacy:*
*Things to Know About Spending and Saving Money*

# Lesson 16: Renting This and Buying That

**$ ACTIVITY PAGE**

## Word list

| | | | |
|---|---|---|---|
| contract | identified | subject | handy |
| term(s) | signature | consideration | formal |
| condition(s) | reverse | thereof | nonconsumable |
| hereby | personal property | acknowledge(s) | |

## Increasing your understanding

1. Look at the word list. If you don't know a word, find out what it means. Try to figure it out from the way it is used on page 47. Or look it up in a dictionary.

2. Supply the missing words from the word list:

  (a) The paper at the top of page 47 talks about contract _____ and conditions.

  (b) The renter who signs the contract _____ and agrees with what it says.

  (c) The renter is _____ by his (or her) signature.

  (d) In the story on page 47, the reporter suggests renting out _____ clothing.

  (e) You can rent out almost anything _____, according to the reporter.

## Questions to discuss

1. Do you think the business person in the story will succeed with Friendly's Rentals? Why or why not?

2. Why are contracts complicated? Do they need to be? Do stores really want you to read all the details in their agreements? Give reasons for your answers.

3. How much should you pay? Imagine that you can buy a sofa, two end tables, a dining room table and four chairs for $1,080. They will last for six years. If you rent the furniture instead, what is the most you can pay each month without losing money? Brainstorm your answers.

## Things to write about

1. What would you rent for a party? Imagine that you are giving a party. What will you want to rent? Write a paragraph giving your ideas.

2. Rewrite the information in the box at the top of page 47. Use your own words, and keep them simple.

## Things to do

1. Role-play the story on page 47 with a partner. Use your own names if you want. Decide on another animal the store might rent out.

2. What are good reasons to rent something? Make a list of at least four.

3. How would you make the rules? Imagine that you and some friends are going to open a video rental store. What will your rules be? Meet with three or four classmates and think of five rules. One can be the price you will charge.

4. What can you rent that's unusual? Look around outside the class. Try the yellow pages or visit a rental store. Then tell your class what you find.

*Life Skills Literacy:*
*Things to Know About Spending and Saving Money*

# Lesson 17: Paying for Health

## Themes

- Preventive health care
- Health insurance

**Background notes:** Learners who are young and healthy with lots of financial needs may not wish to put medical care high on their lists of needs. But they, like the rest of us, should think about such things before problems develop. The best health care dollar may be the one spent to maintain good health—with healthy food or exercise. The next best may be the one spent to avoid health and economic catastrophe—through medical insurance. These pages will help your learners consider such matters and perhaps to move in directions that benefit their bodies as well as their budgets.

## Preparation possibilities

- Think about: health care in your area
- Bring to class: information about health facilities and health insurance

## Technology resources

- Search topic: *health*
- Web pages to try: Health Insight (American Medical Association page)

## Student pages

- Page 50 includes: some quick ideas for maintaining good health, an introductory paragraph about health insurance and preventive medicine, and a story about somebody hospitalized for surgery
- Page 51 includes: a word list you may adjust for your class and student activities

**Especially for ESL:** People new to western culture may need more help than others understanding the laughter expressions incorporated in the story on page 50: *Laughter is the best medicine, I thought I'd die laughing, I laughed so hard I thought my side would split.*

## Extra idioms and slang to introduce

- *Fit as a fiddle:* very healthy
- *Luck out:* be lucky

**Thoughts to share with learners:** Having health insurance is important. If you don't have it now, get it when you can. Be sure to consider health care when you look for jobs.

**Questions to ask learners:** Is health insurance a good thing to spend your money on? What happens if you get sick and have no insurance? What can you do? Do you think the government should provide health care for everybody in the United States? (Or: Do you think the Canadian health plan is a good one?) Do you agree with the last two sentences in the paragraph at the top of page 50? ("Knowing what we should do to protect our health and save our money is often easy. Getting ourselves to do it is the challenge.") Why should this be so?

**Projects to assign learners:** Call or visit a clinic or doctor's office. Ask how much a health exam costs. Call or visit a local hospital. Ask what happens if you are sick and have no insurance. Find some articles about healthy diets and exercise and bring them to class.

**A fascinating fact to share:** In 1995, 39 million Americans could not afford health insurance.

# Lesson 17: Paying for Health

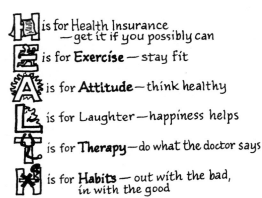

**H** is for Health Insurance
— get it if you possibly can

**E** is for **Exercise** — stay fit

**A** is for **Attitude** — think healthy

**L** is for Laughter — happiness helps

**T** is for **Therapy** — do what the doctor says

**H** is for **Habits** — out with the bad, in with the good

Can you buy good health? Of course not. You can buy good health insurance, and you should if you can. But good health requires more than money. Some of what it takes is shown in the box at the left. Everybody should practice **preventive** medicine. That means doing things to avoid getting sick. Having **physical** exams is one thing you can do. Eating well is another. And getting lots of sleep is a third. Knowing what we should do to protect our health and save our money is often easy. Getting ourselves to do it is the challenge.

$$\$\$\$\$\$\$\$\$\$\$\$\$\$\$\$\$\$\$\$\$\$\$\$\$\$\$\$\$\$\$\$\$\$\$\$\$\$\$\$\$$$

## Story: A funny thing happened

Toshi heard that her friend Nils was sick, and she hurried to the hospital to see him. He was glad to see her.

"A funny thing happened," he told her.

"It doesn't look so funny to me," she said.

"I was feeling kind of down," he said.

"That doesn't sound so funny either," she replied.

"But I heard that laughter is the best medicine. So I went to a comedy show. It was wonderful. I thought I'd die laughing."

"That's good medicine? Then why are you here?"

"That's the funny part. I laughed so hard I thought my side would split. But when I stopped laughing, my side still hurt. It hurt so much I came here. The doctor said I had **appendicitis**, and the next morning I had **surgery**. Funny, isn't it?"

"I think it's terrible, not funny. How can you pay for this?"

"My **HMO** covers it. And this was a real emergency. I didn't even need **pre-authorization** for the **operation**."

"'HMO' means 'health **maintenance organization**,' doesn't it? Do you like having that?"

"It works well for me," said Nils. "Some people like **fee for service** plans better because they have more choice about doctors."

"That's what I have," said Toshi. "But I have a list of **preferred providers**. My share of the cost is less if I go to them. But you look tired, Nils. I should leave."

"Thanks for coming," he said.

"I'll be back," she told him. "Keep smiling."

"I'll smile," said Nils, and he did. "But I can't laugh yet."

"Why not?"

"It hurts too much."

"It won't for very long," said Toshi. "Now get some sleep."

*Life Skills Literacy:*
*Things to Know About Spending and Saving Money*

## Lesson 17: Paying for Health

 **$** ACTIVITY PAGE

### Word list

| | | | |
|---|---|---|---|
| exercise | preventive | HMO | organization |
| attitude | physical | pre-authorization | fee for service |
| therapy | appendicitis | operation | preferred providers |
| habit(s) | surgery | maintenance | |

### Increasing your understanding

1. Look at the word list. If you don't know a word, find out what it means. Try to figure it out from the way it is used on page 50. Or look it up in a dictionary.

2. Supply the missing words from the word list:

   (a) In the story on page 50, Nils had _____ because of appendicitis.

   (b) Toshi pays less for medical care if she goes to _____.

   (c) The paragraph at the top of page 50 says everybody should practice _____ medicine.

   (d) Having _____ exams is one thing you can do to stay well.

   (e) *A* stands for _____ in the list on page 50.

### Questions to discuss

1. Do both people in the story on page 50 have good health? Do you know enough to say?

2. How many good health habits can you think of? Brainstorm your answers for two or three minutes.

3. Is the HEALTH list on page 50 a good one? What does "Think healthy" mean?

### Things to write about

1. How can you get rid of a bad habit? Write a paragraph saying what somebody can do to stop smoking.

2. Imagine that you are Nils in the story on page 50. Write a letter telling your insurance company what happened.

### Things to do

1. Role-play the story on page 50 with a partner. Use your own names if you want. Talk about ways that Nils was lucky and ways he was unlucky.

2. Make another list like the one in the box on page 50. But start with the word FITNESS instead of HEALTH. Do this in a group with three or four classmates.

3. Make a poster telling people to get regular physical exams.

4. Is health care easy to find? Look around outside of class for hospitals and doctors offices in your area. Does your town or city have enough? Share your ideas with your class.

*Life Skills Literacy:*
*Things to Know About Spending and Saving Money*

# Lesson 18: Giving Money and Hours

### Themes

- Giving money to charity
- Volunteering for nonprofit causes

**Background notes:** In 1995, Americans gave more than $1,000 per household to charities and worthy causes. Donations totaled $116 billion, or about 2 percent of the country's personal income. So charity is significant for those who give as well as those who receive. These pages will help your students consider how to give, both well and wisely. They also suggest volunteering as another way of giving, a way that may appeal to learners whose incomes are already stretched by personal and family needs. You might wish to stress that planned giving is often the most effective giving, and that watching for unethical and criminal solicitors is essential.

### Preparation possibilities

- Think about: charities and volunteering in your area
- Bring to class: information about local programs such as United Way

### Technology resources

- Search topic: *philanthropy*
- Web pages to try: National Commission on Philanthropy and Civic Renewal; National Charities Information Bureau; Better Business Bureau Philanthropic Advisory Service

### Student pages

- Page 53 includes: some thoughts about useful giving; an introduction to giving time and money; and a challenge story about giving to charities

- Page 54 includes: a word list you may adjust for your class and student activities

**Especially for ESL:** Ask: How do charities in this country compare to those in your first country? Are some the same? Did you do volunteer work in your first country?

### Extra idioms and slang to introduce

- *Give of yourself:* be generous with your time
- *Handout:* free food or other gift

**Thoughts to share with learners:** Most people who give time and money to others feel good about doing so. You do need to be careful about whom you give to. If you have doubts about an organization, ask the Better Business Bureau about it. If you have doubts about individual solicitors, ask for identification. (See also Activity 3 under "Things to Do" on page 54.)

**Questions to ask learners:** Can you use money wisely and give it away at the same time? What types of charities do the most good? Do the thoughts in the box on page 54 help you answer? Do you agree with them?

**Projects to assign learners:** Choose a charity and find out about it. Make a visit and ask about it. How does it get its money? What does it do with that money? Does it need volunteers? What do they do? Share what you find with the class.

**A fascinating fact to share:** In 1995, Americans gave 20.3 billion hours of volunteer time, according to the National Commission on Philanthropy and Civic Renewal.

# Lesson 18: Giving Money and Hours

*Give people fish, and they can eat a meal. Give people fishing poles, and they can feed themselves.*

Giving money away is easy. But finding the best place to give it is hard. The words in the box suggest giving money where it will do the most good. That might mean finding just the right **charity**. The same is true of **volunteer** hours. You don't want to waste them. But why give away money or hours at all? Most people do it to help others. They aren't rich themselves, but they think others have more problems than they do.

$$$$$$$$$$$$$$$$$$$$$$$$$$$$$$$$$$$$$$$$$$$$$$$$$$$$$$

## Challenge: How much should we give?

**Brother:** Let's talk about our **inheritance**.

**Sister:** What's to say? Let's pay off our bills and take a vacation. The 10,000 dollars that Uncle Henry left us is just about right for that.

**B:** But I think we should give 2,000 dollars away.

**S:** Give it away? Are you crazy? Why?

**B:** Because we're so lucky. Other people need it more than we do. There are lots of good charities around to **contribute** to.

**S:** I say let the rich people be **philanthropists**, not us.

**B:** There are a lot of people poorer than us.

**S:** And some of these charities aren't very good. Half the money they get goes for their own **administration**.

**B:** I know. Some of them **solicit** a lot of money, then spend most of it on **fund-raising**. We'll be careful.

**S:** I want to be careful in Hawaii. We could get there with that money.

**B:** We can still have a nice vacation. Besides, the money we give doesn't all go out the window. The **IRS** will allow tax deductions for our **donations**. We just need to itemize them carefully when we do our taxes.

**S:** I'd rather impress my friends than the **Internal Revenue Service**.

**B:** We can impress our friends when homeless people all have places to sleep.

**S:** I don't mind giving change to the Salvation Army at Christmas. But 2,000 dollars?

**B:** That's impulse giving. We need to plan our giving more.

**S:** I know. Let's **compromise**. Let's volunteer more hours to charity instead of giving all our money away.

**B:** I think we should give more time and money.

**S:** Uh-oh.

**Here's your challenge:** How much of the $10,000 will you give?

*Life Skills Literacy:
Things to Know About Spending and Saving Money*

# Lesson 18: Giving Money and Hours

**($) ACTIVITY PAGE**

## Word list

| | | | | |
|---|---|---|---|---|
| charity | contribute | administration | IRS | Internal |
| volunteer | philan- | solicit | donation(s) | Revenue |
| inheritance | thropist(s) | fund-raising | compromise | Service |

## Increasing your understanding

1. Look at the word list. If you don't know a word, find out what it means. Try to figure it out from the way it is used on page 53. Or look it up in a dictionary.

2. Supply the missing words from the word list:

   (a) In the story on page 53, the second family member wants rich people to be _____.

   (b) The first family member says the _____ will allow tax deductions for donations.

   (c) "Let's _____," says that second member at the end of the story.

   (d) Some charities spend a lot on their own _____.

   (e) The paragraph at the top of page 53 says not to waste money or _____ hours.

---

## Questions to discuss

1. How do you answer the challenge on page 53? What part of their money should most people give to charity?

2. What do people mean when they say "time is money"? Are they right? Is it better to give money or time to a charity?

3. Should the government do what charities do? Why or why not? What would change if the government took over from charities?

## Things to write about

1. What if you inherit $10,000? How will you spend it? Write a paragraph giving your ideas.

2. Can you get people to give? Write a letter soliciting money. Ask readers to help homeless people in your area. Use "Homeless Helpers" as the name of your organization.

## Things to do

1. Role-play the story on page 53 with a partner. Use your own names if you want. Decide on one charity you will give money to.

2. What charities do you like? Make a list of five you will help if you can.

3. How can you know people asking for money won't just use it for themselves? Work with three or four other students. Decide on three or four guidelines for careful giving.

4. What are other people's favorite charities? Ask three or four people outside of class what charities they like best and why. Then share what you find with your class.

*Life Skills Literacy:*
*Things to Know About Spending and Saving Money*

# Lesson 19: Investing Money

## Themes

- Investing money
- Full savings programs

**Background notes:** It may take money to make money, but it doesn't necessarily take very much. Even people new to the workplace and with limited incomes can invest in the stock market and elsewhere. The question is whether they should. These pages introduce learners to the idea that investment should be considered as part of an overall savings program. They suggest retirement as a goal for such a program, and warn that some investments involve risk. They should help your learners understand the stock market as an exciting opportunity to be approached at the proper time with great care.

## Preparation possibilities

- Think about: local courses and seminars in investment and financial planning
- Bring to class: articles and other information relating to investment

## Technology resources

- Search topic: *investment; how to invest; stocks*
- Web pages to try: Fidelity (and other investment houses); Pocket Change Investor

## Student pages

- Page 56 includes: figures showing the results of investing in 1925 (based on statistics in the book *Numbers*, written by Andrea Sutcliffe and published by Harper Perennial in 1996); an introduction to investment and risk; a dialogue about investment as part of an overall financial plan

- Page 57 includes: a word list you may adjust for your class and student activities

**Especially for ESL:** The world of investment has a specialized vocabulary. People with limited English skills should work with an interpreter or an expert who speaks their own language before risking money in it. Ask: Does your native country have its own stock market? Do a lot of people invest in it?

## Extra idioms and slang to introduce

- *Piece of the action:* a share of something, like the profits of a business
- *Put all your eggs in one basket:* risk everything at once; put all your money in one place

**Thoughts to share with learners:** If you have money to invest and want advice, look for an independent counselor. Don't go to somebody who wants to sell you a certain kind of stock. Some people belong to investment clubs and work together to find out about the stock market.

**Questions to ask learners:** Who needs to make financial plans? (Everybody, not just the rich.) What are some elements of financial plans not mentioned in the story on page 56? (Wills and insurance are two.) Does anybody have a lot of interest in the stock market? What can you tell us about it?

**Projects to assign learners:** Call a local stock broker or investment company. Ask how much money you need to buy stock. Visit the company and ask for more information.

**A fascinating fact to share:** The richest person in the world in 1996 was Bill Gates, who founded the Microsoft company. That year his wealth was estimated at $18 billion.

# Lesson 19: Investing Money

## HOW MUCH CAN YOU MAKE?

Here's how money can grow. Imagine you used the money at the left to buy the **stock** of small companies in 1925. How much could that stock have grown by 1993? The figures on the right show that.

| 1925 VALUE | 1993 VALUE |
|---|---|

$1 — $2,757
$10 — $27,570
$100 — $275,700

Do you work hard for your money? That's okay. You can also make your money work hard for you. You can invest it so it will grow. You can put it into savings accounts, and it will earn interest. You can also buy stocks in some companies. Then you own **shares** in those companies. The box at the left shows what can happen if you buy stock. But one thing the box doesn't show is **risk**. Some people invested in bad stocks in the 1920's. They lost all their money. You need to be very careful and talk to experts like stock **brokers** when you invest your money.

$ $ $ $ $ $ $ $ $ $ $ $ $ $ $ $ $ $ $ $ $ $ $ $ $ $ $ $ $ $ $ $ $ $ $ $ $ $ $ $ $ $ $ $ $ $ $ $ $ $ $ $ $

## Dialogue: Getting older

**Druggist:** Hi there, friend. What can I do for you?

**Customer:** Hi. I haven't seen you all week. But I need some pills.

**D:** What for?

**C:** To make me grow old very fast.

**D:** You're always joking around. Why do you want to age quickly?

**C:** I learned in school how much your money can **appreciate** if you buy stocks and keep them a long time. If I invest a hundred dollars now and then grow old, I'll be rich!

**D:** I'm afraid it doesn't work like that. Besides, I'm not sure you should get stock now.

**C:** Why not? I have a friend who invests in a **mutual fund**. That fund buys a lot of different stocks and my friend says it is safe.

**D:** It probably is. But you need to have a whole savings program. You need a cash reserve in case of an emergency. And you need a **retirement** plan.

**C:** Retirement? But I'm not really getting old that fast. And the company where I work doesn't have a retirement plan.

**D:** It's never too early to save for retirement. You save some through **Social Security** but that's not enough. Think about an **Individual Retirement Account.** You can set that up yourself. Any bank can tell you about **IRA's.**

**C:** Maybe I'll ask at Mucho Money Bank. I like it's **slogan**. It says that "More for us is more for you." I like its **logo**, too. It shows one dollar bill turning into 10.

**D:** Choosing a bank because you like its slogan and logo is a terrible idea. You should shop around.

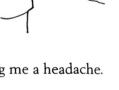

**C:** I suppose so. But before I go, I do need something.

**D:** What can I get you?

**C:** A bottle of aspirin. All this thinking is giving me a headache.

*Life Skills Literacy:*
*Things to Know About Spending and Saving Money*

Name _____  Date _____

# Lesson 19: Investing Money

ACTIVITY PAGE

## Word list

| | | | | |
|---|---|---|---|---|
| stock | broker(s) | mutual fund | Individual | IRA(s) |
| share(s) | druggist | retirement | Retirement | slogan |
| risk | appreciate | Social Security | Account | logo |

## Increasing your understanding

1. Look at the word list. If you don't know a word, find out what it means. Try to figure it out from the way it is used on page 56. Or look it up in a dictionary.

2. Supply the missing words from the word list:

   (a) The figures at the top of page 56 show how the value of _____ can grow.

   (b) One thing figures don't show is _____, says the paragraph at the top of the page.

   (c) A _____ is the first speaker in the story on page 56.

   (d) The customer thinks the Mucho Money Bank has a good _____ and a good _____ .

   (e) The druggist thinks the customer needs a _____ plan.

## Questions to discuss

1. Do you think the druggist in the story on page 56 has a good financial plan? Why or why not?

2. What steps should you take before deciding to buy stock? Brainstorm your answers.

3. What does it mean to own a share of a company? Can you help run the company?

## Things to write about

1. When should people pay for financial advice? How can you choose a good advisor? Write a paragraph giving your ideas.

2. Write a slogan for a financial advisor. Use your own name for the advisor if you want. Or use the name Andrea Able.

## Things to do

1. Role-play the story on page 56 with a partner. Use your own names if you want. Decide what you think the customer in the story should do.

2. What companies would you invest in? Imagine that you have enough money to invest in stock. You want to help the company grow and make money for yourself. List three companies you might invest in.

3. Draw the logo that the story on page 56 describes.

4. Can you find some financial advisors? Outside of class, find the names of five people who can help you with money problems. Then share the names with your classmates.

*Life Skills Literacy:*
*Things to Know About Spending and Saving Money*

57

# Lesson 20: Credit Cards

## Themes

- Using credit wisely
- Understanding credit cards

**Background notes:** Credit cards were first used in 1959. By 1994, the average American carried eight of them. Between the two dates, millions of Americans saluted the convenience the cards offered, and millions more struggled to survive the weight of the debt that use of the cards incurred. Youthful and inexperienced consumers are at particular risk of card-based debts and problems. The cards are easily available (82 percent of college students carry at least one) and easily used to build bills their owners cannot pay in time to avoid hefty interest charges. These pages will help your learners understand credit card dangers and how to avoid them.

## Preparation possibilities

- Think about: your own experience with companies pushing the use of credit cards
- Bring to class: consumer information on the use of credit cards

## Technology resources

- Search topic: *credit cards, Visa* (and similar organizations)
- Web pages to try: The Pitfalls of Plastic Credit Cards; Jump$tart Coalition: Financial Smarts for Students; Credit Card Advisor

## Student pages

- Page 59 includes: part of a credit card billing statement; a brief introduction to credit and credit cards; a story about a financial counselor and a card-holding client

- Page 60 includes: a word list you may adjust for your class and student activities

**Especially for ESL:** Ask: Were credit cards used in your native country? Were they easy to get? Did a lot of people use them?

## Extra idioms and slang to introduce

- *Card:* an amusing person
- *Ten-spot:* 10-dollar bill

**Thoughts to share with learners:** Credit card companies like Visa and MasterCard do not issue credit cards. Banks do. If you lose a credit card, you need to notify the company. You are liable for up to $50 if somebody else uses it. When you use a card, the retailer you buy from pays between 4 and 8 percent to the bank that issued it.

**Questions to ask learners:** Who has received unsolicited credit cards or offers for them? What do you do with such things? If you have two cards, which should you pay first? (The one with the higher interest rate.)

**Projects to assign learners:** Visit a bank and ask about credit cards. Can anybody get them? What interest rate is charged? At the library, look for consumer books. Find out how much it costs to use credit cards. (See books like *The Consumer Bible: 1001 Ways to Shop Smart*, written by Mark Green and published by Workman.)

**A fascinating fact to share:** Arthur Morris introduced the Morris Plan in 1916. It made credit available to working people for the first time. Before then, banks loaned only to the well-to-do.

# Lesson 20: Credit Cards

TERMS and CONDITIONS
For your CREDIT CARD ACCOUNT

ANNUAL **PERCENTAGE** RATE (APR)
9.99%. If payment is received late twice in
any 6-month period, the rate will change to 19.99%.

**GRACE PERIOD** FOR REPAYMENT OF BALANCES
25 days from the date of the monthly statement

ANNUAL FEE
None

**MINIMUM PAYMENT**
2% of the **principal** owed,
but not less than $10.00

GOLD CARD
NEWCITY BANK
3LCG0 314 75

Do you want a credit card? It might be easy to get. In one year, credit card companies sent 2.4 billion letters to consumers. The letters were **unsolicited** offers of credit cards. Some had cards with them. All you had to do was sign the cards and use them. Except for one thing. You also had to pay the bills that came later. If you paid quickly, you owed just for what you bought. But if you paid late, you also owed an interest charge. And the interest could be a lot of money, as many people found out.

$$$$$$$$$$$$$$$$$$$$$$$$$$$$$$$$$$$$$$$$$$$$$$$$$$$$$$$

## Story: A helpful card

Anna and Fred went to see their financial counselor.

"How's it going?" asked Mr. Sung.

"Fine," said Anna. "We've paid off some bills. And we've thrown out most of our credit cards."

"All but one," added Fred.

"Get rid of it," said Mr. Sung. "You know what I think of credit cards. I call them 'the **plastic peril**.'"

"But this one saved our life two days ago," Fred said.

"I don't care what you did with it. You still have to pay for any new debts you **incurred**. That means new interest charges because you already owe a lot."

"But you don't understand," said Anna.

"I understand the credit card business," Mr. Sung told them. "The companies are so **aggressive** they send you **preapproved** cards whether you want them or not. They offer **perks** like free airline miles to get you **hooked**."

"We know," said Fred. "You showed us that before. We were making minimum payments

on the cards. You proved that we were going to pay more than $1,300 for $1,000 worth of furniture. You said the banks would love that."

"They sure would. Their rates are so high it's almost **usury**."

"That's why we keep hearing musical radio **jingles** saying credit cards are great," said Anna. "Those ads cost a lot, but they are worth it to the bank."

"That's for sure," said Mr. Sung. "Look, credit cards can be great conveniences. But they require lots of discipline. They don't work well for you two."

"We agree," said Anna. "We know you are right."

"Then why did you use a card two days ago? And how can you say it saved your life?"

Fred laughed. "We used it to scrape the frost off our car windows," he said. "It worked great. And they can't charge us interest for that."

*Life Skills Literacy:*
*Things to Know About Spending and Saving Money*

# Lesson 20: Credit Cards

$ **ACTIVITY PAGE**

## Word list

| percentage | minimum | plastic | aggressive | hook(ed) |
| grace period | payment | peril | preapprove(d) | usury |
| unsolicited | principal | incur(red) | perk(s) | jingle(s) |

## Increasing your understanding

1. Look at the word list. If you don't know a word, find out what it means. Try to figure it out from the way it is used on page 59. Or look it up in a dictionary.

2. Supply the missing words from the word list:

   (a) The minimum charge for the card at the top of page 59 is 2 percent of the _____ owed.

   (b) The _____ is 25 days from the date of the statement.

   (c) In the story on page 59, Mr. Sung calls credit cards "the _____ _____."

   (d) Anna talks about hearing radio _____ that cost a lot.

   (e) Perks like free airline miles can get you _____ on credit cards, according to Mr. Sung.

## Questions to discuss

1. What does Mr. Sung mean by "plastic peril" in the story on page 59? Do you think he's right about credit cards?
2. How can you decide if credit cards are good for you to use?
3. What are some good and bad points about credit cards? Brainstorm your answers.

## Things to write about

1. Are there ever good reasons to charge something? Answer in a paragraph or two.
2. Imagine that you lose a credit card. Write a letter to Your Card Company telling them what happened. Make up your own facts.

## Things to do

1. Role-play the story on page 59 with a partner. One of you can be Fred or Anna. The other can be a financial counselor. Use your own names if you want. Decide if Fred and Anna are good financial planners.
2. How much do you owe? Imagine that you have a credit card. Its terms are the same as the ones in the box on page 59. One month the principal you owe is $450. Figure out the minimum that you must pay.
3. Can you get people to use Pepe's Plastic Credit Card? Write a radio jingle to convince them. Then sing it or read it to your classmates.
4. How many ads can you find for credit cards? Look around outside class. Then share your answer with classmates.

*Life Skills Literacy:*
*Things to Know About Spending and Saving Money*

# Lesson 21: Warranties and Complaints

## Themes

- Warrantee protection
- Complaining when things go wrong

**Background notes:** There's a touch of ironic inevitability associated with faulty products. They tend to be the things we have wanted most, saved for longest, and researched best. There's also a touch of predictability to product and purchase problems: They will happen to all consumers sooner or later. These pages will help your learners plan and prepare for such events by considering such things as warranties and the steps they should follow when things go wrong. Consumers do have rights that are carefully protected by law in many cases. But benefiting from the rights often requires personal initiative and action.

## Preparation possibilities

- Think about: local consumer assistance agencies and small claims courts
- Bring to class: news reports of consumer complaints and case settlements

## Technology resources

- Search topic: *consumer complaints, small claims courts* (both by state or province)
- Web pages to try: State of California, Department of Consumer Affairs, Complaint Mediation Division

## Student pages

- Page 62 includes: a brief discussion of the steps consumers should follow when they have problems with purchases; a challenge story about warranties and extended protection plans
- Page 63 includes: a word list you may adjust for your class and student activities

**Especially for ESL:** People new to the English language may be more reluctant than others to complain when things go wrong. Simple role-plays around topics like making returns could be helpful to them.

## Extra idioms and slang to introduce

- *Grin and bear it:* accept a problem without complaining
- *Take it on the chin:* be defeated

**Thoughts to share with learners:** Many consumer affairs experts think extended protection plans are a bad deal for customers but a great deal for stores. Stores offer three different types of return policies: exchange (of a similar item), return for credit, and refund. Many, but not all, stores today have liberal returns policies so that customers will be satisfied and keep coming back.

**Questions to ask learners:** What does it mean to say that "The squeaky wheel gets the grease"? (People who complain get help.) Do you find it hard to complain when you have a problem? What can you do about that?

**Projects to assign learners:** Visit a small claims court. Watch a session if you can. Get complaint forms to share with the class. Find out how much you can sue for in a small claims court. (Often up to $2,000. Anything larger must be handled in civil court, and you will usually need a lawyer for that.)

**A fascinating fact to share:** Every year, more than 28 million Americans are injured by consumer products, not including automobiles. That's according to *Consumer Reports* for November, 1994.

# Lesson 21: Warranties and Complaints

What can you do if something you buy has a problem? Try these steps:
- Complain to the store.
- Complain to the manufacturer. Call or write a letter.
- Call or write your newspaper or TV station.
- Complain to the Better Business Bureau.
- Complain to the government.
- Go to **small claims court**. You won't need a lawyer.

Keep all your receipts and warranties. Send copies with written complaints. Don't give up. Complain until the problem is fixed.

$$$$$$$$$$$$$$$$$$$$$$$$$$$$$$$$$$$$$$$$$$$$$$$$$$$$$$$$$$$$$$$

## Challenge: Extra Protection

**Customer:** I want to buy this boom box. It sounds great.

**Salesperson:** It should. At $175 it's our very best small box.

**C:** And it's **guaranteed** as long as I live, right?

**SP:** Not quite that long, I'm afraid.

**C:** But your sign says "lifetime guarantees."

**SP:** That **applies** to the boom box, not you.

**C:** You mean the boom box is guaranteed until it dies?

**SP:** You could put it that way.

**C:** But what if it dies tomorrow?

**SP:** It won't. But if it's **faulty**, it's covered by our full limited 90-day warranty. If you are **dissatisfied** in any way, just bring it back in its **original carton** and show **proof of purchase**.

**C:** But what if a part goes bad in six months?

**SP:** The manufacturer will replace **defective** parts for a year.

**C:** And after that I'm out of luck?

**SP:** If you have a **legitimate** complaint, just come in and we'll **resolve** it.

**C:** You'd better, or I'll see you in small claims court.

**SP:** There's no need to **threaten** anything like that.

**C:** I'm not making a threat. I'm making a promise.

**SP:** I have a better idea. Why not consider our extended protection plan? It's the best in the industry. It protects your boom box for 36 months. If it breaks, we fix it. No questions asked. Unless you do something stupid, of course. Like dropping it in a lake.

**C:** Why would I do that?

**SP:** I can't think of any good reason. But let's talk about the plan. As you say, this boom box is expensive. Maybe you should protect your investment.

**C:** Okay. What's the bad news? How much for the plan?

**SP:** Just $24.95 for the full three years.

**Here's your challenge:** Imagine that you are the customer. Do you buy the plan?

*Life Skills Literacy:*
*Things to Know About Spending and Saving Money*

# Lesson 21: Warranties and Complaints

## Word list

| | | | |
|---|---|---|---|
| warranties | guarantee(d) | original | legitimate |
| extended | applies | carton | resolve |
| protection | faulty | proof of purchase | threaten |
| small claims court | dissatisfy(ied) | defective | |

## Increasing your understanding

1. Look at the word list. If you don't know a word, find out what it means. Try to figure it out from the way it is used on page 62. Or look it up in a dictionary.
2. Supply the missing words from the word list:

   (a) The store in the drawing on page 62 says it has the best lifetime _____.

   (b) You won't need a lawyer in _____, says the list at the top of page 62.

   (c) In the story on page 62, the salesperson says the store will _____ any legitimate complaint.

   (d) The manufacturer will replace _____ parts in the boom box for a year.

   (e) If you want to bring something back, you should put it in its _____.

## Questions to discuss

1. How do you answer the challenge on page 62? Do you get the extended protection plan? Are such plans usually a good idea?
2. What does this saying mean: *Let the buyer beware.* Do you agree with it?
3. What does this saying mean: *The customer is always right.* Do you agree with it? How does it compare with the saying in question 2?

## Things to write about

1. Have you ever had a problem with something you bought? Write a paragraph telling the story.
2. Can you get action? Imagine that you buy the boom box in the story on page 62. It breaks in two weeks, but the store won't take it back. The manufacturer won't help, either. Write a letter to the consumer protection office of your state. Tell what happened, and ask for help.

## Things to do

1. Role-play the story on page 62 with a partner. Use your own names if you want. Talk about some other questions the customer should ask.
2. What should a warranty cover? List four problems you expect the warranty for a boom box to cover. (One might be faulty parts.) List four more problems you don't expect a warranty to cover. (One might be getting it wet.)
3. Can you sell service? Make a poster advertising extended protection plans for Happy Harry's Boom Box Store.
4. How often do people complain about things they buy? Outside the classroom ask three or four friends or family members if they ever complain to stores. Tell your class what you learn.

*Life Skills Literacy:*
*Things to Know About Spending and Saving Money*

# Lesson 22: Taxes

## Themes

- Understanding and accepting taxation
- Keeping adequate tax records

**Background notes:** "In this world nothing can be said to be certain, except death and taxes," said Ben Franklin. But at least one more thing is fairly certain: the fact that many people fail to plan adequately for either of the first two. These pages will help your learners to understand the importance of Franklin's second certainty to their own lives, and to recognize the need for keeping records and otherwise preparing in advance for tax deadlines. The pages also introduce the topic of audits and the possibility of getting professional assistance when dealing with tax matters.

## Preparation possibilities

- Think about: local and state or provincial tax laws affecting your students
- Bring to class: tax forms and instructions

## Technology resources

- Search topic: *taxes* (by geographic area and political entity)
- Web pages to try: Yahoo! Tax Center; Yahoo! Canada Tax Centre, TaxWeb
- Software to consider: Kiplinger TaxCut, Taxbyte (Canadian), programs for calculating, paying income taxes

## Student pages

- Page 65 includes: the introductory section of a U. S. income tax form, a brief introduction to taxation, and a dialogue between an auditor and a taxpayer. Note that the form includes some terms that might not be familiar to learners; most of these are highlighted elsewhere on the page.

- Page 66 includes: a word list you may adjust for your class and student activities

**Especially for ESL:** People new to the United States and Canada seeking to understand taxation might appreciate a review of various governments and their taxing powers. Say: Most local, county, state or provincial, and national governments have taxing powers. Ask: How do taxes in your new country compare to those in your first country?

## Extra idioms and slang to introduce

- *Penny pincher:* a stingy person
- *Cash cow:* something (like a business) that produces a lot of money

**Thoughts to share with learners:** Many people have good experience dealing with tax agencies. But some do not. The IRS and other agencies do make mistakes that cause serious problems for some people. If you think this is happening to you, you may need to get help from a lawyer. The IRS audits some people because it thinks there might be a problem, and some others at random.

**Questions to ask learners:** What taxes do we pay in this area? State income tax? A sales tax?

**Projects to assign learners:** Get some tax forms and instructions from a bank or post office. Bring them to class to share. With your classmates, decide who would use each one.

**A fascinating fact to share:** About 5 percent of the people audited by the IRS get refunds. Most end up owing money.

# Lesson 22: Taxes

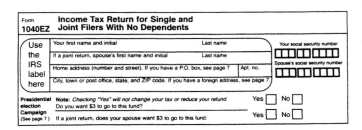

Some people don't like what's in the box. It's the top of a federal **tax return**. This form is for **single** and **joint filers**. You can use it alone. Or you and your **spouse** can use it together. People with children or other **dependents** need another form. Millions of **taxpayers** file forms like these every year. If you are prepared, the job is easy. If you aren't ready, it can be tough. How do you prepare? You should keep good records. You should get tax forms early. If you need help with the forms, you should get that early, too.

$ $ $ $ $ $ $ $ $ $ $ $ $ $ $ $ $ $ $ $ $ $ $ $ $ $ $ $ $ $ $ $ $ $ $ $ $ $ $ $

## Dialogue: The tax **audit**

**Taxpayer:** I'm here for my audit.

**Auditor:** Come in. And please relax.

**T:** I can't. Look, my hands are shaking.

**A:** All of you is shaking. Why don't you put your wheelbarrow in the corner and sit down?

**T:** Thanks.

**A:** What's in the wheelbarrow?

**T:** My records. And some money. If I lose this fight I might have to pay a **penalty**.

**A:** But this isn't an **adversarial** meeting. We aren't enemies, and we don't need to fight.

**T:** Don't you work for the **Infernal** Revenue Service?

**A:** It's "Internal," not "Infernal." "Infernal" means awful.

**T:** I'm sorry. I know what "infernal" means. My uncle used to call it that. I'm sorry. I really am.

**A:** That's okay. Now let's review your tax records.

**T:** What can be wrong? Hasn't my boss been **withholding** the right amount of pay for taxes?

**A:** That looks fine to me.

**T:** One year I was sick and missed the April 15 deadline. But I asked for an **extension** and got it. Wasn't that okay?

**A:** Of course. That's **routine**.

**T:** And I've always done my own taxes. Maybe I should have gone to a **Certified Public Accountant**.

**A:** A **CPA** isn't necessary for you. Another adviser might have helped, but that's not what you really need. I think you need a different form.

**T:** I've always used the 1040EZ.

**A:** I know. But you have seven children.

**T:** That's right. Four girls and three boys.

**A:** Then you do need a different form. You have a lot of deductions to take. I think the government owes you some money.

**T:** That's wonderful. Can I get it today? I've got room in my wheelbarrow.

**A:** Not today, I'm afraid. But we can figure things out today. Then we can send a check very soon.

*Life Skills Literacy:*
*Things to Know About Spending and Saving Money*

## Lesson 22: Taxes

### Word list

| | | | |
|---|---|---|---|
| tax return | spouse | penalty | extension |
| single | dependent(s) | adversarial | routine |
| joint | taxpayer(s) | infernal | Certified Public |
| filer(s) | audit | withhold(ing) | Accountant (CPA) |

### Increasing Your understanding

1. Look at the word list. If you don't know a word, find out what it means. Try to figure it out from the way it is used on page 65. Or look it up in a dictionary.

2. Supply the missing words from the word list:

   (a) The form in the box on page 65 is part of a federal _____.

   (b) People with children or other _____ can't use that form.

   (c) "But this isn't an _____ meeting," says the auditor in the story on page 65.

   (d) The taxpayer's employer has been _____ the right amount of money.

   (e) The taxpayer asks about going to a _____, or CPA.

### Questions to discuss

1. What's wrong with paying too much income tax? How could the taxpayer in the story on page 65 have avoided that?

2. Do you pay too many taxes? Why do you feel as you do?

3. What's the fairest tax? Is it better to have income taxes? Or sales taxes? Or is there some other type of tax that's better? What do you think?

### Things to write about

1. How do you like to learn about complicated things like taxes? If you have a question do you read a book? Talk to somebody? Use the Internet? Write a paragraph about your learning style.

2. Can you get people to file taxes early? Imagine that you work for the government.

You want people to pay taxes early. That way, your work won't all come in at once. Write a radio slogan asking people to file early.

### Things to do

1. Role-play the story on page 65 with a partner. Use your own names if you want. Talk about why the taxpayer is nervous.

2. What do your taxes do for you? Make a list of at least seven good things that taxes pay for.

3. What should taxpayers do? With three or four classmates, write four guidelines to help taxpayers. One might be: Keep records of expenses and deductions.

4. How much tax help can you find? Look around outside of class for books and advisers to help with taxes. Tell your class what you learn.

*Life Skills Literacy:*
*Things to Know About Spending and Saving Money*

# Lesson 23: In Time of Trouble

## Themes
- Dealing with debt problems
- Considering bankruptcy and Debtors Anonymous

**Background notes:** Debt is like illness. The best way to deal with it is to prevent it. But that's not always possible. These pages will help learners consider some of the options available when financial problems mount. One solution may sound better to some students than it really is, and that is personal bankruptcy. Consider telling your learners that bankruptcy is a good option for some people, but it comes at considerable cost. Credit, self-image, and reputation all can be lost in bankruptcy proceedings. Take care, also, in your discussions of Debtors Anonymous. Avoid any questions or comments that would cause loss of anonymity for students or others with experience in this or similar programs like Alcoholics Anonymous.

## Preparation possibilities
- Think about: local bankruptcy laws and collection practices
- Bring to class: information about bankruptcy laws, local financial counselors, Debtors Anonymous groups

## Technology resources
- Search topic: *debt collection, credit repair*
- Web pages to try: Debtors Anonymous, American Debt Collection

## Student pages
- Page 68 includes: an ad for a financial counselor, a brief introduction to financial problems, and a story about a man in a debt management crisis

- Page 69 includes: a word list you may adjust for your class and student activities

**Especially for ESL:** Ask: What do people in your native country do when they have money problems? Can they declare bankruptcy? Do many people do that?

## Extra idioms and slang to introduce
- *Strong-arm:* involving the use or threat of force
- *Deliver the goods:* do what you promise

**Thoughts to share with learners:** Bankruptcy might sound good to some people. You don't have to pay some bills, and you get a fresh start. But you also lose your credit rating and hurt your reputation. The Fair Debt Collection Practices Act puts strict limits on bill collectors. If you tell a bill collector in writing not to communicate with you any more, the bill collector can get in touch just one more time. If you ever do that, send your letter by certified mail so you can get a receipt.

**Questions to ask learners:** What would you expect if you went to a meeting of Debtors Anonymous? (It works like Alcoholics Anonymous to help all sorts of people do better with their money.)

**Projects to assign learners:** Find out if there are Debtors Anonymous groups in this area. Find out where to complain if you are hounded by a debt collector. (You might try calling the local district attorney's office.)

**A fascinating fact to share:** Nearly one million Americans file for personal bankruptcy every year.

# Lesson 23: In Time of Trouble

Somebody loses a job. Somebody else has too many bills to pay. One person's rent goes up, and somebody else gets sick. What can we do when money problems pile up? Financial counselors can help. They can suggest ways to work with our **creditors**, the people we owe money to. They know what bill collectors can and can't do. And they know what's good and bad about bankruptcy. If you think you need a counselor, go soon. Waiting won't help.

$$$$$$$$$$$$$$$$$$$$$$$$$$$$$$$$$$$$$$$$$$$$$$$$$$$$$$$$$$$$$$

## Story: Taking Control

Samuel Sung's new client was Abner Spender. He had big problems.

"My company closed and I lost my job for two months," he said. "Now I have a better one. But my mother is sick and the bills have piled up. A bill collector called me at midnight Tuesday. He said he would **repossess** all my furniture, even my mother's bed."

"That's **harassment**," said Mr. Sung. "It's a **violation** of the law."

"But how do I stop him?"

"The next time he calls, talk about the Fair Debt Collections **Practices Act**. That's a federal law. He'll stop if he thinks you know the law. If he doesn't, we'll make a complaint to the attorney general."

"Then should I file for bankruptcy? So I can forget my bills?"

"Let's try to avoid that. You'll wreck your credit record. And you'll have to pay for some things like student loans and taxes and **child support**. Do you have any of those?"

"I owe a lot of taxes."

"Bankruptcy won't solve that. Tell me, do you have **chronic** payment problems or is this something new?"

"It's just since I lost my job. I usually pay all my bills on time. And I always spend my money very carefully."

"Good. I often tell people with chronic problems about **Debtors Anonymous**. That group helps people who always seem to have lots of **overdue** bills. But you don't need that. You need to work out a payment plan. I can help with that. Then you can talk to your creditors about it. Many companies will wait for payment when they know you are trying hard."

"That's great, Mr. Sung. Can we do that at our next meeting? I have to go now."

"Okay. Big plans for tonight?"

"I promised my girlfriend an expensive dinner out. This is her birthday."

"I see."

CONSUMER HELP
M·E·N·U
Common Sense
Bankruptcy
Counseling
Credit Card
Control
Discipline
Budgeting
Saving

*Life Skills Literacy:*
*Things to Know About Spending and Saving Money*

## Lesson 23: In Time of Trouble

ACTIVITY
PAGE

### Word list

| | | | | |
|---|---|---|---|---|
| collector(s) | creditor(s) | violation | child support | Debtors |
| bankruptcy | repossess | practice(s) | chronic | Anonymous |
| consultation | harassment | act | | overdue |

### Increasing your understanding

1. Look at the word list. If you don't know a word, find out what it means. Try to figure it out from the way it is used on page 68. Or look it up in a dictionary.

2. Supply the missing words from the word list:

   (a) In the story on page 68, Mr. Sung asks if Abner has _____ payment problems.

   (b) Bankruptcy won't help with bills for some things, including _____.

   (c) A group called _____ helps people who keep having credit problems.

   (d) You get a free _____ if you go to Samuel Sung, according to the ad at the top of page 68.

   (e) Samuel Sung can help when the bill _____ start calling.

### Questions to discuss

1. At the end of the story on page 68, Mr. Sung says, "I see." What do you think he sees? Explain your answer.

2. Why are there bankruptcy laws? When people and businesses say they are bankrupt, they don't have to pay some bills. Is this a good idea? Who does it help? Who can it hurt?

3. How can friends help each other get over money problems? Brainstorm some answers.

### Things to write about

1. What kind of person makes a good financial counselor? Write a paragraph with your ideas.

2. Can you get a bill collector to stop bothering you? Imagine that your roommates bought a TV set you didn't want. They took the TV with them when they moved. But a bill collector says you owe $800 for the set. Write a letter telling the collector not to call you again.

### Things to do

1. Role-play the story on page 68 with a partner. Use your own names if you want. Talk about what you think will happen next.

2. How can people get out of financial trouble? List four rules for people who have too much debt. One of them might be: Throw away your credit cards.

3. Can you convince people to get financial counseling? Imagine that you and two or three classmates are financial counselors setting up a business together. Make a plan for telling people about your work. How will you advertise? What will you say in your ads? Make notes about your ideas so you can share them with your whole class.

4. Can you find a bankruptcy sale? Sometimes when businesses go bankrupt, banks sell their property. Look in local newspapers to see if there are any sales in your area. Can anybody go and buy things?

*Life Skills Literacy:*
*Things to Know About Spending and Saving Money*

# Lesson 24: Learning More

## Themes

- Finding information about using money wisely
- Judging information about using money wisely

**Background notes:** How many decisions does a single paycheck represent? The answer is very high. There are the employment, government and business decisions affecting the check. Then there are the personal decisions about where the money could go. Too many decisions to count, and too many to do each and every one perfectly well. But for every economic decision we make, from where to get a haircut to what stock to buy, information is available to help us. The trick is to find it and evaluate it. These pages will help your learners begin to consider how to find information beyond that offered by this *Things to Know* package and how to judge it.

## Preparation possibilities

- Think about: library and other local consumer resources
- Bring to class: copies of *Consumer Reports*, other useful consumer guides

## Technology resources

- Search topic: *consumer guides* (products, services by name)
- Web pages to try: *Consumer Reports*; LawChek; The Law Library

## Student pages

- Page 71 includes: guidelines for making consumer decisions; a paragraph about getting and evaluating consumer information; a challenge activity about purchasing a camera
- Page 72 includes: a word list you may adjust for your class and student activities

**Especially for ESL:** Learners may be able to offer each other information about where to find consumer and financial information in their first language. Ask: Where did you get product and other consumer information in your first countries?

## Extra idioms and slang to introduce

- *Take something with a grain of salt:* Be doubtful about some information
- *Bad mouth:* Say bad things about someone or something

**Thoughts to share with learners:** These pages talk mostly about product information. But much of what they say is also true of other financial information—getting health care, for example, and investing money. People who provide information and have no reason to care about your decision are called "impartial sources." *Consumer Reports* magazine is a good example of an impartial source.

**Questions to ask learners:** Think about the last five dollars you spent. How did you decide what to spend it for? Did you do any research? Do you now wish you had? Where would you look for information?

**Projects to assign learners:** Choose a product. Then visit a local library and write down the names of some books or magazines about that product. Also, write down the names of three general books or magazines written for consumers.

**A fascinating fact to share:** A piece of paper money is also called a *note.* The largest note issued by the U. S. government is for $100,000. It is used only by the Federal Reserve and the Treasury Department.

# Lesson 24: Learning More

*Do you know enough to use your money wisely? Maybe you want to buy a camera, but you don't know much about them. If that's the case, here's what you can do:*

**L**ook for all the information you can get.

**E**valuate all the information you find.

**A**nalyze the information

**R**evise your own ideas

**N**egotiate a better deal based on your new information

Lots of people will tell you what to do with your money. But the person who counts the most is you. It's your money, and you can use it poorly or wisely. But how do you know? How can you tell what to do? Some answers appear in the box at the left. Also, remember this rule: Never take advice at **face value**. Always evaluate what you hear. What's in it for the people giving the advice? Will they get your money if you spend it the way they suggest? That's not necessarily bad, but it's always something to consider.

$ $ $ $ $ $ $ $ $ $ $ $ $ $ $ $ $ $ $ $ $ $ $ $ $ $ $ $ $ $ $ $ $ $ $ $ $ $ $ $ $ $ $ $ $ $

## Challenge: What should I get?

**First Friend:** I want to buy a **camera** with my birthday money. What do you think I should get?

**Second Friend:** I don't have the slightest idea. I don't know anything about cameras.

**FF:** Thank you for being honest. You're the first person who has said that.

**SF:** I didn't know you were interested in **photography**.

**FF:** I want pictures of the party this weekend. So I thought a **single-use** camera would be okay. That's just 10 dollars at Freda's Photo.

**SF:** Sounds reasonable to me.

**FF:** But Freda said a good **compact** camera might be better. Then I could use it again and again.

**SF:** I bet it costs more. Have you evaluated that idea? The way we talked about in consumer ed class?

**FF:** It costs 40 dollars. And yes, I know Freda will make more money if I spend more. But that doesn't mean it's a bad idea.

**SF:** The compact camera might be better for the **environment**, too. Who else have you asked?

**FF:** Some friends. One is a good photographer. She says to get a **single-lens reflex**. That's an even better camera. It costs about a hundred dollars new. But she has a used one I can buy for 65.

**SF:** Do you think what she says makes sense? Maybe you need to read some consumer magazines to see.

**FF:** I'll do that at the library tomorrow.

**SF:** Then maybe you need to **rethink** what you want. Or do you want to really try photography as a **hobby**?

**FF:** I don't know. That's the hard part.

**SF:** And once you do all your **research**, maybe your friend will come down in her price.

**FF:** But if I get the cheap camera, I'll have a lot more money left. I just don't know.

**Here's your challenge:** Imagine that you are the first friend. What will you do?

*Life Skills Literacy:*
*Things to Know About Spending and Saving Money*

# Lesson 24: Learning More

## Word list

| evaluate | face value | single-use | single- | hobby |
| revise | camera | compact | lens reflex | research |
| negotiate | photography | environment | rethink | |

## Increasing your understanding

1. Look at the word list. If you don't know a word, find out what it means. Try to figure it out from the way it is used on page 71. Or look it up in a dictionary.

2. Supply the missing words from the word list:

   (a)  The sign at the top of page 71 says to _____ all the information you find.

   (b)  After you get some information, you should _____ your own ideas.

   (c)  "I didn't know you were into _____," says the second friend in the story on page 71.

   (d)  The first friend might buy a _____ camera from another friend.

   (e)  The paragraph at the top of page 71 says not to take information at _____ .

## Questions to discuss

1. What's your answer to the challenge on page 71? What's the best deal for you?

2. Do the friends in the story follow the LEARN guidelines on page 71? Explain your answer.

3. How can consumers learn about cameras? Brainstorm some ideas.

## Things to write about

1. Is a single-use camera a good idea? What is good about it? What is bad? Write your ideas in a paragraph or two.

2. Where have you gotten some good advice about using your money? Make a list of three or four places. Then write a sentence about each one.

## Things to do

1. Role-play the story on page 71 with a partner. Use your own names if you want. Decide where else the first friend might look for information.

2. Can you add to the LEARN list? Read the LEARN list on page 71 again. Then, with two or three classmates, think of three things to add so that LEARN turns into LEARNING.

3. Draw a picture to illustrate the story on page 71.

4. Where do most people get advice about what they are buying? From friends? From the people who sell them? Ask three or four people outside of class where they get advice. Then share what you find with your class.

*Life Skills Literacy:*
*Things to Know About Spending and Saving Money*

# Slang and Idioms

# Answers

## Words for completing sentences:

Page 3: (a) resources; (b) in debt; (c) lottery; (d) charge cards, take charge; (e) spendthrift

Page 6: (a) co-op; (b) KISS; (c) discipline; (d) liabilities; (e) balance

Page 9: (a) categories; (b) detective; (c) miscellaneous; (d) savings account; (e) net worth

Page 12: (a) furnished; (b) nonsmokers; (c) protect; (d) security deposit; (e) illegal

Page 15: (a) relations; (b) candle; (c) lease; (d) interest, delinquent; (e) account number

Page 18: (a) buy, in bulk; (b) specialty; (c) consumption; (d) supermarket; (e) convenience

Page 21: (a) checkouts; (b) impulse buying; (c) temptation; (d) calories; (e) appetites

Page 24: (a) retail; (b) irregulars, imperfects, seconds; (c) nonprofit organizations; (d) impress; (e) interview

Page 27: (a) cost-effective; (b) hail a cab; (c) peak; (d) ticket book; (e) disabled

Page 30: (a) financial; (b) transferred; (c) overdrawing; (d) hock; (e) debit card

Page 33: (a) Web Site; (b) dedicated; (c) health plan; (d) reserved; (e) specialist, consultant

Page 36: (a) economics; (b) discretionary; (c) incidentals; (d) advertisers; (e) benefits

Page 39: (a) gimmick; (b) competition; (c) accused; (d) Preferred; (e) promotions

Page 42: (a) advantages; (b) bargains; (c) employment, agency; (d) fraud; (e) attorney general

Page 45: (a) amateur leagues; (b) culture; (c) radical; (d) open rehearsals; (e) programs

Page 48: (a) terms; (b) acknowledges; (c) identified; (d) formal; (e) nonconsumable

Page 51: (a) surgery; (b) preferred providers; (c) preventive; (d) physical; (e) attitude

Page 54: (a) philanthropists; (b) Internal Revenue Service (IRS); (c) compromise; (d) administration; (e) volunteer

Page 57: (a) stock; (b) risk; (c) druggist; (d) slogan, logo; (e) retirement

Page 60: (a) principal; (b) grace period; (c) plastic, peril; (d) jingles; (e) hooked

Page 63: (a) warranties; (b) small claims court; (c) resolve; (d) defective; (e) original carton

Page 66: (a) tax return; (b) dependents; (c) adversarial; (d) withholding; (e) Certified Public Accountant

Page 69: (a) chronic; (b) child support; (c) Debtors Anonymous; (d) consultation; (e) collectors

Page 72: (a) evaluate; (b) revise; (c) photography; (d) single-lens reflex; (e) face value

## Math problems

Page 15: Number 3 under "Things to do": $2.60 for 4 hours; $67.60 for a year

Page 48: Number 3 under "Questions to discuss": $15 (which equals the cost per month of the purchase)

Page 60: Number 2 under "Things to do": $10.00